The Politics of Juridification

T0347552

The *Politics of Juridification* offers a timely contribution to debates about how politics is being affected by the increasing relevance of judicial bodies to the daily administration of Western political communities. While most critical analyses portray juridification as a depoliticizing, de-democratizing transferral of political authority to the courts (whether national or international), this book centres on the workable *ambivalence* of such a far-reaching phenomenon. While juridification certainly intensifies the power and competences of judicial bodies to the disadvantage of representative political institutions, it cannot be easily reduced to the demise of democratic politics. By focusing on the multiple ways in which social agents make use of the law, *The Politics of Juridification* teases out the agential and transformative aspects of the various negotiations social agents engage with legal institutions with a view to obtaining political visibility. In particular, the book homes in on two seemingly distinct phenomena: on the one hand, the regulation of sexuality and emerging kinship formations; on the other, the fragmentation of legal settings due to the claims to legal autonomy advanced by sub-state cultural and religious groups. By doing so, the book makes the case for an unexpected convergence between the struggles for legal recognition of sexual minorities and religious and cultural minorities. The conclusion is that juridification does entail normalization and favour the infiltration of law into the social realm. Yet because of its ambivalent nature, it can and does serve as an alternative vehicle for social change – one that attaches more importance to how social agents produce law on a daily basis and how this law permeates official legal orders.

Mariano Croce is Assistant Professor of Political Philosophy at Sapienza Università di Roma, Italy. His research includes theory of the state, legal and political institutionalism, legal pluralism and LGBTQIA studies. Among his books are *The Legal Theory of Carl Schmitt* (Routledge, 2013, with A. Salvatore) and *Undoing Ties: Political Philosophy at the Waning of the State* (Bloomsbury Academic, 2015, with A. Salvatore).

Part of the

LAW AND POLITICS:
CONTINENTAL PERSPECTIVES

series

Series Editors
Mariano Croce, *Sapienza University of Rome, Italy*
Marco Goldoni, *University of Glasgow, UK*

For information about the series and details of previous and forthcoming
titles, see https://www.routledge.com/law/series/LPCP

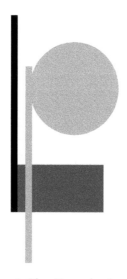

A GlassHouse book

The Politics of Juridification

Mariano Croce

Routledge
Taylor & Francis Group

LONDON AND NEW YORK

First published 2018 by Routledge

2 Park Square, Milton Park, Abingdon, Oxfordshire OX14 4RN

52 Vanderbilt Avenue, New York, NY 10017

Routledge is an imprint of the Taylor & Francis Group, an informa business

First issued in paperback 2019

British Library cataloguing in publication data
A catalogue record for this book is available from the British Library

Library of Congress cataloging in publication data
Names: Croce, Mariano, author.
Title: The politics of juridification / Mariano Croce.
Description: Abingdon, Oxon [UK] ; New York : Routledge, 2018. |
    Series: Law and politics : continental perspectives |
    Includes bibliographical references and index.
Identifiers: LCCN 2017047605| ISBN 9780415750134 (hbk) |
    ISBN 9781315795720 (ebk)
Subjects: LCSH: Law—Political aspects. | Legal polycentricity. |
    State, The. | Justice, Administration of—Political aspects.
Classification: LCC K487.P65 C79 2018 | DDC 340.9—dc23
LC record available at https://lccn.loc.gov/2017047605

ISBN: 978-0-415-75013-4 (hbk)
ISBN: 978-0-367-28023-9 (pbk)

Typeset in Times New Roman
by Swales & Willis Ltd, Exeter, Devon, UK

Contents

Acknowledgements

This book has benefited from the support of a large number of colleagues and friends over the last five years. I have had longstanding conversations, which in one way or another affected the contents of this book, with Petr Agha, Daniele Archibugi, Stefano Bancalari, Laura Bazzicalupo, Lorenzo Bernini, Marco Bontempi, Caterina Botti, Marina Calloni, Thomas Casadei, Sandro Chignola, Davina Cooper, Dimitri D'Andrea, Massimo De Carolis, Donatella Di Cesare, Piergiorgio Donatelli, Alessandro Ferrara, Olivia Guaraldo, Martin Loughlin, Fiona Macmillan, Emmanuel Melissaris, Gianfranco Pellegrino, Stefano Petrucciani, Andreas Philippopoulos-Mihalopoulos, Alain Pottage, Nello Preterossi, Ingrid Salvatore, Aldo Schiavello, William Twining, Marco Ventura, Lars Vinx, Marc de Wilde, and Lea Ypi. They all have nurtured a marvelous environment of questioning and research. I want to express special thanks to Frederik Swennen, as we have been developing together the 'cont(r)actualization' project. A big thanks goes to those who comprise my closest environment: Virginio Marzocchi, Andrea Salvatore, Michele Spanò, and Valeria Venditti. I am deeply grateful to Marco Goldoni for his staunch support of all my projects. I am just as grateful to Colin Perrin, who makes things happen. I also want to thank all those at Routledge who provided considerable help and advice. Finally, for the organization of many events where I had the opportunity to present and revise my work, I want to acknowledge the financial support of the project awarded by Charles University Primus/Hum/15 'Transformation of law in post-national contexts'.

Introduction

1 The legal circuit and the process of conversion

The law is a strange kind of knowledge. An artificial 'as if' that makes things happen. However, as Yan Thomas (1995) points out, it is not so much the 'as if' that should strike us as the relation it entails between legal categories and reality – law's moving away from facts as a possibility condition for it to operate on facts. It is a subversive attitude to facts, Thomas insists. Law claims to re-order things, to remould the order in which they are assembled. This is because law is first and foremost a *technique of description* that provides guidance for conduct precisely insofar as it describes. Thomas deftly captures this trait as he accounts for law's operational mode as one that I would like to call 'obliquity'. It is a movement whereby law's performative force does not address the object directly, but affects it obliquely, by attending to something else. The way in which Roman law concerned itself with religious things, he writes, epitomizes such an oblique attitude of the legal technique. His essay on that special form of *res religiosa* that is the tomb shows how little Romans were interested in the religious aspect of the issue. '[I]n the Roman world the category of religion was rationalised in such a way as to facilitate the development of rules which were ultimately concerned with the disposition of worldly goods, with ownership and exchange' (Thomas 2004: 68). The production of a legal category relating to worldly goods, ownership and exchange occurs indirectly, as a strictly legal operation instituting a basic separation between that which the law can talk about and that which it cannot. The law attached particular prohibitions to particular objects, for these things to be granted a special status of inviolability and inalienability. Yet, by doing so, it instituted a lexicon that would allow dealing with the property of the dead without any 'trace of some belief, metaphysics, or idealisation relating to the world of the deceased' (Thomas 2004: 67–68).

In sum, only superficially did the Roman legal category at issue concern the set of things that could not be sold or exchanged, while it was meant to produce a technique for the management of inheritance funds. As it dealt with religious things, Roman law was carving out a certain space not concerned with beliefs and mental habits, but with inheritance transactions. More generally, this is but an example of how, according to Thomas, the legal technique works: law is concerned with its own categories and only with them, while its reference to the world is always a form of self-reference. This is how the law subsumes things obliquely – by addressing the things whose regulation implicitly regulates that which is not directly regulated. A transverse regulation instituting that which is *not* taken into account, what is left in the field of legal speakability without it being openly mentioned. The law drags a particular object within the legal field without this object being directly addressed. The obliquity of indirect definition is suspended on a legal vacuum with no substantive ground. It is the effect of procedures by which legal words determine their own boundaries with respect to non-legal entities and establish what falls within its regulatory scope. In this de-substantivized proceduralism, the legal language is not isomorphic to the world, as it opens up a *semiotic field* where the world can be described in such a way that it should fit legal categories. The legal direction of fit is always world-to-word.

This portrayal entails a specific conception of the law as a technique of description that claims non-legal reality should always fit legal categories. Elsewhere (Croce 2012; Croce 2014) I elaborated on this aspect to pinpoint some of the characteristics that make the law the particular normative order it is. I advanced a conception of the law as neither a rule-based practice nor a well-defined territory. Law is a specific type of trans-sectional knowledge that claims to be self-sufficient on account of its own insulated categories, elaborate rituals and formulaic language. 'Self-sufficiency' emerges as law's constitutive claim not to be dependent on anything which is outside the legal. This is a claim that Pierre Bourdieu (1987) deems to be the core of the juridical field. He explains that legal descriptions, definitions, prescriptions and provisions override the descriptions, definitions, prescriptions and provisions of other normative practices by dint of legal knowledge being independent of the knowledge of everyday life as well as the specific knowledge of other social fields. In brief, the law attains normative pre-eminence over other kinds of normativity thanks to a circular recourse to its (claimed) self-sufficiency. Law's own autonomy is presented as the basis of its independence from extra-legal factors and thus its ability to play as a third party in the conflicts that arise in society.

While law's claim to self-sufficiency is just a claim, the whole legal edifice is conditional on it. As I noted, it has to do with law's working along an oblique line that need not address reality directly. As Bruno Latour comments, the only goal of law is

> to connect texts with facts and with other texts. . . . The judge, if she is honest, will say that she has settled the 'legal truth' but not the 'objective' truth in the case at hand. . . . she will cite the Latin adage according to which the judgment is *pro veritate habetur* ('taken as the truth'): neither more nor less.
>
> (Latour 2013: 54)

Yet, it is imperative not to mistake this view for a sceptical account of legal truth as something artificially constructed. More interestingly, what lies behind this conception is 'a processual vision of law', as Kyle McGee (2015: 474) puts it, 'insofar as the obligations must be constructed before they are satisfied, and the satisfaction of one is the construction of the next'. In this sense, there is nothing behind or beyond the law but its semiotic repertoire and the possibility it offers of partaking in its processes. The legal knowledge is first and foremost a web of special signs that permits reframing in legal terms questions that people in everyday life verbalize with recourse to ordinary language and solve with the normative resources of other (non-legal) rule-governed contexts. This is the reason why legal truth's being insensitive to other regimes of truth institutes a *circuit*: a place where facts and events are remoulded and reordered by means of a circular interplay with legal categories. At the same time, it is much more than a simple construction, as it is an account of facts and events with enforceable effects that act back on the social with remarkable force.

At this stage, it is worth stressing two points. First, the legal technique of description does not intend to alter the meaning of something that has really happened; let alone to distort or deform facts. Inside the semiotic circuit, the very category of the factual represents an artefact – one that serves as the intellectual vehicle for the processual production of legal truth. At the same time, legal truth is not an end in itself but is intended to produce effects on what lies outside the legal field. Second, legal truth comes about as the outcome of a semiotic replacement: as legal categories take the place of ordinary language, the former ignite a productive circularity between the facts brought into the legal field and the legal language that has to yield a legal account of them. In short, the law's special stock of knowledge is that which enables people to discuss and solve conflicts within an extra-ordinary domain, in which special categories are at work. Therefore, what is crucial to the law is the way in which people interact with each other and speak about conflicts within the legal circuit. This explains why this book will not so much pay heed to the constructedness of legal categories or the special relation they have with social reality, as to the way people use them.

The concept of 'law-user' was advanced by Laura Nader in the context of her 'user theory of law' – one that deems the law 'to be made and changed by the cumulative efforts of its users' (Nader 1984: 952). As such, it is a methodological orientation attuned to the role of *social agents who use the law*. Agents are as relevant to the life of the law as the courts or judicial decisions because 'use or non-use patterns' prove a major determinant of institutional change (Nader 2002: 49–51). The direction of law largely depends on who is motivated to use the law and for what purposes. This is why, from a methodological standpoint, social agents are given equal sociological significance to all the players who partake in the legal process. Certainly, the use of this methodological approach to the agents' doings within the legal field which I will make will not take law-users to be strategic actors who intentionally use legal institutions to achieve clear-cut objectives. While this strategic orientation is most often present and manifest, I will concentrate on the interplay between law's obliquity and the agents' recourse to law. This interplay cannot be considered as a straightforward, transparent relation between a limited range of users (those who actually use law for specific purposes) and the legal institutions that are involved. As I will argue in this book, the effects of use or non-use patterns extend to a much wider range of people and noticeably impinge on the more general understanding of what law is and what it is expected to do.

To put it another way, a user theory of law – as I understand it here – places emphasis on the various ways in which the movement of people who make use of legal means yield effects on reality. In particular, what interests me in people's recourse to the law's special knowledge is that the effects it engenders are to be attributed to how people *invoke, use and misuse legal categories to account for the facts they are concerned with*. By relying on law's stock of knowledge and special language, people – under the guidance of legal proxies – commit themselves to forging a paradigm of argument that is supposed to lead to a sharable account of the relevant facts in terms of one or more implicit or explicit normative referents (see Comaroff and Roberts 1981: 92–93). In this way, the language of everyday life is replaced for the legal language. The knowledge of other fields is used for legal purposes and consequently gets incorporated into the legal knowledge. The rules of non-legal normative contexts are replaced for the rules of law. People turn out to transcend both their personal views of things and to place themselves into the semiotic circuit that transforms the conflict. Therefore, in the oblique way that characterizes legal processes, the outcome of the processual production of legal truth acts back on how people perceive what is outside the semiotic circuit.

It is in view of the particular role the law plays that the autonomy of the legal and the self-sufficiency of its knowledge have to be preserved. In order for the processual truth to exert its effects, legal descriptions, definitions, prescriptions and provisions are to be perceived as the outcome of an independent, autonomous and self-sufficient activity carried out within a bounded venue. This allows a process to take place which is one of the law's key tasks: by employing legal categories and the legal language, under the guidance of experts, everyday reality can be renegotiated by those (laypeople) who transitorily cross the borders of the legal field. But just because the independence and self-sufficiency of legal categories are instrumental in this task, legal knowledge is inevitably refractory to revision and amendment. Change in the legal field is meticulously administered by a set of rules, procedures and rituals, which are a core element of law. Therefore, law's distinctiveness and oblique productivity comes at a cost. While the parties are bound to comply with a restricted and stable set of categories to provide entirely new accounts of facts, these categories become the vehicle of the description that produces the effects people are seeking. As I will explain throughout the book, this ignites a looping effect whereby the legal categories that are conjured to account for certain facts affect the identity and self-perception of those who mobilize those categories. This book's main objective, however, is to show that there are ways of using law that remarkably reduce law's obliquity and even promote creative transformations in the body of law.

2 Traditional politics and the politics of juridification

The short discussion above paves the way for the analysis I will carry out in this book. Its core is how the law affects what it does not address directly. I intend to pursue this line of inquiry by homing in on some of the ways in which particular societal dynamics are being altered and shaped by people's recourse to law. However, before providing a few details on how the book unfolds, it is worth introducing an orthogonal theme that makes this analysis relevant to the conceptualization of the relationship between law and politics. The specific manner in which the law carries out its job is all the more significant at a time in which politics is receding and is gradually making room for an intensification of people's recourse to legal means. It is what scholars call the 'juridification' of society (see, for example, Teubner 1987; Blichner and Molander 2008; van Waarden and Hildebrand 2009; Magnussen and Banasiak 2013). As I understand it here, juridification exceeds by far the expansion of legal competences in channelling social change or the transfer of authority to judicial institutions. It is not a merely institutional process that registers an expansion in the scope of legal bodies and the redistribution of competences and authority. As Jean and John Comaroff (2009: 33) comment, it is a more general paradigm shift in the juridico-political culture lumping together seemingly unrelated phenomena:

> Whereas post-Second World War constitutions stressed parliamentary sovereignty, executive discretion, bureaucratic authority and cultural homogeneity, recent ones focus, if unevenly, on the primacy of civil and political rights, the freedoms of the citizen, the limitations of state power, the tolerance of difference, and the rule of law.

To recall a felicitous, pithy formula that gives a sense of this paradigm shift, '[c]lass struggles seem to have metamorphosed into class actions' (Comaroff and Comaroff 2006: 27). Class actions here are but the flagship of a novel juridico-political setting where the legal technique becomes a vehicle for social actors to verbalize and reframe their culture, race, sexual orientation, faith and habits of consumption as law-users.

According to the Comaroffs, there is no societal sphere that is not being juridified due to the global spread of neoliberal capitalism, which heightens the grounding of citizenship in the jural. This is because, they argue, contemporary societies (both in the West and outside the West) are increasingly being infiltrated by a liberal, contractarian conception of one's life and one's relationships that sanctify 'free' markets and its commodification of everything (Comaroff and Comaroff 2003). They regard the law as both an instrument and a vector of this process. They are not the only scholars who envisage a link between liberal law and juridification. For example, in an empirically grounded essay on this phenomenon, Gad Barzilai (2007) maintains that liberalism is naturally inclined to grant the law a prominent role because of its two basic principles; namely, the preference accorded to individual rights over other types of collective good, and the neutrality of procedural justice, which is to be attained through professional knowledge of the legal framework. Barzilai does not provide a strictly relist or elitist reading of this phenomenon, but draws our attention to law's being a technical language mastered by specialists. In a way that resonates with my discussion above, it is the semiotic structure of the law that juridifies all that enters its orbit, and, as I insisted, also what lies outside.

While the liberalizing and privatizing inclines identified in these and other studies are undeniable, I think there is much more to juridification. The use of law does not simply entail the production of self-interested, market-responsive individual and collective subjects. The use of law is also conducive to the creation and actualization of new connections that activate new forms of political action. This is why I reject the view that juridification brings about the straightforward withdrawal of politics and the depoliticization of social struggles. Rather, it is a kind of politics that is carried out *within* and *through* the courts – and even *outside* them. While this book's aim is not to analyze the dynamics and outcomes of this politics, I would like to foreground its form – one that is implanted on a particular relationship between institutional language and ordinary language. The main contention I will make is that juridification is a form of politics that yields visible and less visible effects because of law's obliquity.

For there is no doubt that traditional politics within and without institutions – whether it is representative politics or movement politics, petitions, protests, strikes, upheavals – rests on an interplay between the language of institutions and the language of everyday life different to the one the legal circuit requires and enacts. In this regard, Bourdieu's analysis of how political action works can be of help. He maintains that politics is first and foremost the creation of links between social agents with a view to forming groups and to giving specific configurations to the social world. Politics entails a 'work of representation' which makes groups speakable and socio-politically visible as political units (e.g. the notion of class that is meant to unite workers as they come to class consciousness; or the more recent revival of religious faith as a fundamental identity marker of substate groups). In brief, the political work of representation is

> the capacity to make entities exist in the explicit state, to publish, make public (i.e., render objectified, visible, and even official) what had not previously attained objective and collective existence and had therefore remained in the state of individual or serial existence – people's malaise, anxiety, disquiet, expectations – represents a formidable social power, the power to make groups by making the common sense, the explicit consensus, of the whole group.
>
> (Bourdieu 1985: 729)

It is a form of representation as it gives a visible, objective shape to something that would not otherwise exist as a recognizable entity of its own. Still, it is not a creation *ex nihilo* (see Croce and Salvatore 2017). Whether it is the outcome of party politics carried out inside and outside institutional arenas or other forms of social struggles, politics as the constitution of political units has an objective and a subjective side. On the objective side, social agents exhibit certain properties that, once they are combined in light of a specific 'principle of pertinence', supply the material base for the constitution and maintenance of the group. On the subjective side, in order that groups may come about and be visible, these properties must be combined as they independently are not conducive to any specific configuration of the social. In other words, the political work of representation is that which allows the agents to

> discover within themselves common properties that lie beyond the diversity of particular situations which isolate, divide and demobilize, and to construct their social identity on the basis of characteristics or experiences that seemed totally dissimilar so long as the principle of pertinence by virtue of which they could be constituted as indices of membership of the same class was lacking.
>
> (Bourdieu 1991: 130)

On this understanding of politics, the relationship between the work of representation and the identity of a group does not amount to a purely symbolic construction; nor is it the mere ostension of factual commonalities among social agents. Political struggle revolves around the possibility of *saying the social world* in ways that change it by assembling its elements in keeping with rival principles of pertinence. Put otherwise, politics is a permanent conflict between competing modes of saying the social world. Political transformation is based on a 'symbolic destruction' of existing allegiances and the construction of new ones that foster alternative visions of the social.

Bourdieu's conception, however, does not elide either the agential element or the innovative force of politics. It is because of the concurrence of an objective and a subjective side that people contribute significantly to configuring the social. Whether their political actions are crafted as demands addressed to their parliamentary representatives or whether these actions take the shape of extra-institutional undertakings, they are part and parcel of an activity of ongoing critique of the very representation that produces the groups. People's mobilization challenges the available lexicon as it sets the stage for a critique of the social taxonomies that are attached to the dominant way of saying the social. In other words, whether it is institutional or extra-institutional (although this is certainly more evident in the latter type of politics), politics brings into question the social schemes that are at the root of social injustice and paves the way for the imagination of alternatives. Politics enables a 'heretical subversion' that is meant to change 'the world by changing the representation of this world which contributes to its reality' (Bourdieu 1991: 128). Bourdieu conjures the notions of 'paradoxical pre-vision' and 'utopia', in the sense that political action always works as a 'pre-vision' that intends to actualize what it utters.

This is a striking difference with the politics of juridification, as I will argue throughout this book. To make my case, I will pursue a twofold objective. While I will claim that juridification occasions important forms of political action, I will also foreground what it entails in terms of questioning the existing institutional lexicon. The main argument will be that people's using the law politically hardly allows questioning the lexicon they build on to raise their claims. As Bonnie Honig (2009: 79) has it, 'law cannot be pressed into new directions unless claims . . . are made in its name and using its terms'. This is a crucial aspect of using law as a political weapon. Needless to say, while legal knowledge and categories are not impermeable to what lies outside the legal field, change in them occurs through procedural channels that are already and always *legally* regulated. Facts and events are brought into the legal only if they are reconstructed in compliance with legal knowledge and categories and are adjudicated by means of a discursive operation. Contrary to traditional politics, the language and categories of everyday life scarcely turn out to effect a heretical subversion. Facts and events have to be translated into the language and categories of the law by professionals who master legal knowledge. It is a 'process of conversion' – 'the conversion of a direct struggle between parties into a dialogue between mediators' (Bourdieu 1987: 830) – whereby the specialized language of the law prevails over the others. Legal experts filter the discursive contributions of laypeople in order for them to be brought in line with the categories featuring in legal texts. Settling a dispute entails framing the facts at stake in such a way that they might fit the legal categories into which they have to fall.

It is no use expanding on this aspect in the context of this Introduction, as it will be the main focus of the book. Yet, it is worth insisting that the analysis of juridification requires a two-faced theoretical attitude. On the one hand, a non-reductionist approach that teases out the innovative and transformative potential of using law. Law-users are not passive agents stealthily governed by opaque rationalities; the legal circuit feeds off ongoing negotiations that are carried out by laypeople who enter the legal field to make claims that are more and more political in nature. On the other hand, the lexicon of law is not the lexicon of politics, as entering the legal field requires endorsing legal categories and knowledge as they allow replacing the language of everyday life with the legal language. Because of law's innate tendency to regulate obliquely, the effects on what is not at stake in legal disputes are enormous. More generally, the effects of law as it becomes a major source for affirming one's identity are profound and incisive. This is what this book aspires to bring to light.

3 Juridification: within and without institutions

As Alec Stone Sweet (1999) reminds us in his influential study on judicialization, judicial power has a prototypical triadic structure. It is meant to settle the conflict between two disputants under the guidance of a dispute resolver. The triad, Stone Sweet continues, is instrumental in the preservation of the dyad, in the sense that the presence of a third party – the dispute resolver – makes sure that the disputants never resort to violence to settle their dispute (see also Stone Sweet and Grisel 2017: 11–20). At present, a good deal of studies document an increase in people's reliance on the judiciary and the adjudication process as an efficient form of governance (see, for example, Tate and Vallinder 1995; Shapiro and Stone Sweet 2002; Hertogh and Halliday 2004). While judicialization often reaches the acme of the juridico-political and involves constitutional bodies – as the latter are called upon to review acts of the legislative and executive branches (Forsyth 2000; Robertson 2010) – it is not confined to the lofty level of constitutional law.

Ran Hirschl (2008) has offered a detailed picture of the various aspects of judicialization. Not only does it dominate the justice system, from civil procedure to criminal justice, but it also permeates key policy areas such as family, education, public health, industrial relations, consumer protection, immigration, taxation and many others. This is why judicialization is but an aspect of juridification, understood as a more general process whereby the law comes to affect social relations. Indeed, Hirschl remarks that a striking feature of recent judicialization is that judges are more and more involved in what he calls 'mega-politics', that is, core political issues that cut into the identity of a political community – from electoral processes to the prerogatives of state powers, from macroeconomic planning to national security, up to key issues relating to 'collective identity, nation-building processes and struggles over the very definition – or *raison d'être* – of the polity as such' (Hirschl 2008: 123). This is what leads him to speak of 'juristocracy'. Interestingly, this trend is not explained as an invasive clutch of courts over politics but as 'a convenient refuge for politicians to avoid or delay unwanted political outcomes' (Hirschl 2008: 15). In other words, it is politics that counts on the language of law, its instruments and technicalities, to duck its traditional tasks. If this is the case, Hirschl is right when he observes that this type of judicialization is far more disruptive than the over-exercise of judicial review commonly known as 'judicial activism'. Courts' supplementary activity in the field of mega-politics does not stem from the 'intrusion' of judges into the political. The transition to juristocracy is first and foremost a political, not a juridical, phenomenon (see Hirschl 2006: 754) originated by the awareness that politics is less effective and efficient than the law and its agencies.

However perceptive this account may be, it differs from mine in one major respect. This book will not centre on the greedy expansion of the judicial or the pusillanimous retreat of politics, but on how people (mostly laypeople) are the engine of judicialization. Accordingly, my focus will be on how law-users mobilize legal categories, the consequences of this mobilization, and how legal institutions react to it. In a few words, my main argument will be that juridification should be understood as the overexpansion of the legal field as the venue where a variety of struggles are carried out, ones that in the past would be regarded as quintessentially political.

In this regard, John Comaroff has advanced the intriguing notion of 'theo-legality' as a movement towards the sacredness of the legal that goes beyond the West and turns into a distinguishing mark of contemporary constitutional states throughout the world. Theo-legality epitomizes 'the rising salience of the law – at once as ideology, as species of practice, as utopic cure-all, as landscape of political struggle, as instrument of governmentality' (Comaroff 2009: 194). While Comaroff's analysis dovetails in some important respects with Hirschl's, the former insists on law being fetishized as it defines new 'privatized' collectives. People's recourse to law assigns them a 'segmental' identity. As I will illustrate in the various sections of this book, people's achieving particular goals is conditional on them acquiring these identities through law. This explains the 'tendency of populations defined by, among other things, faith, culture, gender, sexual preference, race, residence and habits of consumption to turn to jural ways and means in order to construct and represent themselves as "communities"' (Comaroff 2009: 197). In short, today's juridification should not be simplistically interpreted as merely hinging on institutional dynamics; in that recourse to law, judicialization and lawyering are becoming sites 'of collective action in the context of dynamics in political power and public discourse' (Barzilai 2007: 254).

It is this specific connection between the use of law and the constitution of new collectives that I would like to foreground. I intend to unearth the two sides of the politics of juridification – one that occurs within courts and another that takes the shape of a resistance to state law. In doing so, I would like to make the point that juridification does not only take place within judicial contexts, because it is the much broader social phenomenon that Comaroff speaks of. While law-users who have recourse to official state law enter the semiotic circuit and operate on reality through legal categories, other populations seek to escape the clutch of state law and invoke legal autonomy. In either of these scenarios, law-users are active legal operators as they embark on various processes of conversions that change what lies outside the cases at issue.

Chapter 1 will discuss how the language of rights is affecting the very idea of citizens' relation to the law. By doing so, it will also cast some light on the way rights produce specific types of subjectivity through a 'looping effect'. Rights are the vehicle for legal categories that confer legal speakability on *social* agents and hence render them into *legal* agents. My objective is to shed some light on the *ambivalence* of juridification.

Law empowers but converts, recognizes but alters, opens to some and closes to others. This is the predicament of the politics of juridification, whose effects are always oblique. While the law recognizes some populations as right-bearers, it affects their identity (in visible and less visible manners) as well as the identity of other populations who are not involved in the legal case. The chapter focuses on lesbians', gays' and bisexuals' claims to legal recognition of their unions, and more generally on how the transformation of family and kinship practices is being tackled by the law. My intention is to follow the movements of law-users and to take note of the effects they produce. As far as sexuality is concerned, I will contend that reliance on law has led to momentous social conquests but has also reinforced the conjunction of the signifiers comprising the traditional family grid (mainly based on faithful, committed, long-lasting, dyadic love).

What concerns me in this form of juridification – that which occurs within official courts – is the law playing a decisive part in the remoulding and reordering of the social. Law's claim to self-sufficiency, its categories and its formulaic language become a site of identity-making that makes sense of Judith Butler (2004: 105) speaking of 'desiring the state's desire', as '[t]he state becomes the means by which a fantasy becomes literalized: desire and sexuality are ratified, justified, known, publicly instated, imagined as permanent, durable' (Butler 2004: 111). Along a similar line, Marc Galanter's (1981) analysis of the relation between official law and indigenous orderings resonates with Thomas' conception of law as he explains how official law radiates messages and symbols that informally regulate what is outside the legal field. He shows how subjects who operate in 'the shadow of the law' tend to pre-adapt to official legal standards with no previous (open and coercive) pressure on the part of official institutions. For law plays a restorative effect on social reality which is key to the existence itself of social order.

As far as the issues discussed in Chapter 1 are concerned, the looping effect which connects social conducts to ratified and legitimized legal standards implies a sort of self-modelling. Previously abject sexual relationships enter the field of admissible sexuality by carrying out a twofold activity. The moment same-sex people lay claims to legal recognition, they accept that the issue of same-sex sexuality will be almost entirely reframed in terms of the available legal standard (though revised to accommodate new forms of unions). Yet, acquiring legal speakability, as Michael Warner's (1999) famous critique makes clear, has a series of exclusionary consequences. He writes that marriage 'is never a private contract between two persons. It always involves the recognition of a third party – and not just a voluntary or neutral recognition, but an enforceable recognition' (Warner 1999: 117). Warner's reference to enforceability calls attention to how the law affects the shape and contents of a practice. His is certainly not a plea for restricting marriage to different-sex couples. Rather, his point is that framing the issue of same-sex sexuality discrimination in terms of claims to official recognition of same-sex marriage reinforces legal marriage's 'selective legitimacy' (Warner 1999: 82) whereby the state gets to 'regulate the sexual lives of those who do not marry' (Warner 1999: 96).

The oblique character of legal regulation comes to the surface under the guise of a selective legitimacy that makes something speakable to the detriment of that which remains unspeakable. Nonetheless, this book will not pursue this more critical line of enquiry. I will not concern myself with how institutions work as governmental devices that allocate speakability and distribute advantages. Instead, I will look at how this distributive mechanism of symbolic and material privileges is set in motion by the activity of law-users as they invoke the law to attain specific goals. In this sense, I see the 'normalization' that Warner denounces as not so much an institutional effect; I mainly see it as the outcome of the way in which social actors use legal means.

Chapter 2 will highlight this agential factor from a reverse angle. A movement that is not towards the legal but (at least apparently) goes in the opposite direction. In fact, at present more and more small and less small collectives seek to acquire autonomy from the law of the state. On the one hand, social agents bring into question consolidated historical-political patterns that led to the formation of constitutional states, and do so in a way that – as I will insist – revive the practical side of religion. On the other hand, however, I will point out that the vehicle for their claim-making is, again, the legal lexicon. As Davina Cooper (2014: 27) observes, even as people argue for the pluralization of legal orders, 'there nevertheless remains a powerful tendency to draw the paradigm of law (what law actually means so one can know when it is present) from state law'. Although, as I will illustrate, not all types of legal pluralism are modelled on state law, Cooper makes a point when she draws attention to the debt of new conceptual lines to dominant conceptual frameworks. When religious groups and other types of groups put the accent on the constructed character of hierarchies between legal and non-legal normativities and challenge the pre-eminence of state law, often it is the image of law that I described at the beginning that is at work. Against this involuntary reliance on the dominant legal lexicon, Chapter 2 will identify ways of conceiving the plurality of legal orders that escape such a conceptual trap. In this sense, the principal objective of Chapter 2 will be to understand how the obliquity of the law can be lessened in order to temper its less visible effects. Therefore, while the revival of religion and legal pluralism can unexpectedly turn out to buttress the dominant position of the state legal system – even when they overtly contest it – it is the stress on what people do within practical contexts that casts light on a more creative politics of juridification, one that is likely to contribute to a new composition of law and politics. Indeed, it is my conviction that the only way to tame the transverse effects of legal regulation is to actualize multiple (even competing) contexts of normativity where people enact various identities according to their position in those contexts.

In conclusion, the politics of juridification is a Janus-faced phenomenon that should neither be dismissed as the downfall of democracy nor exalted as the dawn of a spontaneous, harmonious stateless order. My analysis of the politics of juridification remains conscious of the oblique effects of the law as a technique of description, but gives credit to unpredictable uses that vitalize law-users' agency. I believe it is its ambivalence that should be emphasized, especially the one that characterizes the activities of people when they try to attain political goals through legal means. Paying due heed to this ambivalence – this is the book's chief claim – allows identifying unexpected sites of committed politics that, although less disruptive than traditional heretical subversion, is likely to lead to a new, more efficient composition of law and politics.

Some of the contents included in this book have appeared in different form elsewhere. Chapter 1 draws from materials published as 'Homonormative Dynamics and the Subversion of Culture', *European Journal of Social Theory*, 18(1) (2015): 3–20; 'From Gay Liberation to Marriage Equality: A Political Lesson to be Learnt', *European Journal of Political Theory*, published online before print 16 April 2015, DOI: 10.1177/1474885115 581425. Chapter 2 draws from materials published as 'Secularization, Legal Pluralism and the Question of Relationship-Recognition Regimes', *The European Legacy* 20(2) (2015): 151–165.

1 Juridification within institutions
The law of sex and kinship

This chapter is concerned with how the law is serving as a semiotic circuit where the basic notions of sexuality, family and kinship are currently being revised. In this sense, I will look not so much at the legal instruments that are being deployed by legislatures and courts to accommodate a variety of sexual lifestyles and family formations, as at the use of them that is being made by social actors who ask for legal recognition. Not only does this understanding avoid objectivist pitfalls whereby the role of social actors is effaced and the law figures as a top-down machinery driven by barely visible forces. More than that, this view emphasizes the central role that social agents are granted by contemporary legal techniques. In brief, this chapter is devoted to showing how the law *juridifies by empowering* those who have recourse to it. At the same time, it unearths some of the most remarkable socio-political effects of this juridification dynamic.

The core of this analysis will be what it takes for marginalized and excluded forms of sexuality and kinship to obtain what I call 'legal speakability'. This can be described as the entrance of social agents into the legal field in order for them to make claims and negotiate rights with a view to changing their position within the social domain. The law functions as a potent mechanism of socio-political visibility as it redresses the conditions of those who suffer from a situation of social marginalization and whose voice fails to reach out to the sphere of politics. As I will illustrate, this mechanism presents us with undeniable efficacy. The examples of same-sex rights, same-sex marriage and new parenting figures will showcase the success of legal battles. However, I will make the claim that socio-political visibility through legal means comes at a price. The activity of filtering carried out by the law changes the categories by which people perceive and describe themselves. To do this, the Section 1.1 delves into the striking change undergone by same-sex rights claims. Section 1.2 critically discusses the subverting potential of new kinship formations. Section 1.3 casts some light on one of the typical strategies through which the law operates as a sieve that preserves some models of relationships and excludes others. While this is an old chestnut in legal and political theorizing, what I want to discuss here is how and to what extent this aspiration reinstates the legal lexicon as a privileged site of identity-making.

1.1 The legal boundaries of admissible sexuality

In the last few decades, the regulation of sexual conduct and sexual relationships has been at the centre stage of social and political debates. Western societies or, more precisely, Euro-American (Strathern 2005) socio-cultural understandings of kinship and sexuality have undergone so profound a change that at present the constitutive elements of their lexicon (such as family, marriage, parenthood and many others) hardly conjure up the same images that they did 50 years ago. Other elements of kinship will be discussed later in this chapter, but there is no doubt that the main features of the Euro-American sexual imagery have been resignified (Butler 1997; Lloyd 2007; Croce 2015b). For widespread intuitions and values attached to sex and gender have been drastically revisited. The lines of conventional binaries (such as man/woman, male/female and straight/gay) have been blurred and a basic instability is believed to characterize the sphere of people's sexuality. The rapid spread in many fields (from society at large to academia) of the term 'queer' is exactly intended to denote the vagueness of sexual categories and the multiplicity of sexual orientations.

To be sure, this is one of the most relevant transitions of our epoch, whose political, legal and social import is yet to be fathomed. As argued by David Schneider (1980; 1984), the initiator of so-called 'new kinship studies' (see Section 1.2), the sexual imagery, as well as the vocabulary of kinship that it nurtures, are nothing other than a set of 'cultural units' deeply ingrained in a society's symbolic universe. These cultural units operate as cognitive instructions that social actors produce to make sense of their environment and that they are called upon to follow as they take on specific roles within social practices. Therefore, alterations in such a cognitive background result in alterations in the way social actors interact with each other and understand their own place in the world. Whether one views these alterations as an increase in tolerance and acceptance of (once despised) expressions of sexuality or – as a variety of critics whose position will be discussed shortly claim – as a redefinition of the boundaries that separate the natural from the pathologic and the respectable from the abominable, newly enacted policies on sexuality are redefining a crucial aspect of both people's self-perception and public life. But how is this process unfolding?

Certainly, a crucial push for change was the legalization of same-sex sexuality and the recognition of same-sex unions. Not unlike kinship, the history of same-sex sexuality is a history of cultural units. Mariana Valverde (2006) suggests that these units are scarcely firm and permanent, as they are exposed to unpredictable changes. Michel Foucault's (1978) ground-breaking investigation into the emergence of homosexuality as a specific identity category pinpointed a historical shift from a view of homosexuality as a range of acts (sodomy), which were not associated to stable types of subjectivity, to a view of homosexuality as a specific form of identity based on natural factors (for nuanced analyses see also Weeks 1990 and Halperin 2002; for a comprehensive account see Löfström 1997). Such a naturalization of homosexuality and the corresponding congealment of a set of acts into an identity category allowed homosexuals to become the subject of a variety of knowledges in both the fields of hard and social sciences. Valverde points out that today this identity category is being superseded. With the demise of comprehensive socio-political struggles and the rise of post-identity politics, the category of 'the homosexual' no longer serves as an epoch-making cultural unit. Lately the unit that is being used as a weapon to effect momentous social change is the *respectable homosexual couple*.

On the one hand, this reflects the broad change of attitudes I have illustrated at the outset. In today's Euro-American socio-cultural environment attraction to people of the same sex is much less stigmatized, while many lesbians, gays and bisexuals can be utterly open about their relationships and sexual preferences (I would like to note that I will use the acronym 'LGB' and will not mention other variations that include transgender, queer, and intersexual people because the historical as well as legal trajectories of these groups differ in some important respects from lesbian, gay, and bisexual ones – see in particular Stryker 2008). National and international media favourably portray same-sex interactions, while opinion surveys attest to growing social tolerance and acceptance towards LGB sexualities and their concerns. On the other hand, though, such cultural advances are deeply marked by the unit that has supplanted the category of the homosexual – the couple – that is accompanying the accommodation of same-sex rights and thus is shaping the new faces of state policies on family and kinship. How did this remarkable shift come about?

I believe this shift is a revealing instance of the more general process of juridification that, as I explained in the Introduction, is one of the hallmarks of the contemporary junction between the legal and the political spheres. William Eskridge (2013) effectively foregrounds how LGB people have moved from 'outlaws' to 'in-laws'. I suggest that this shift should not be regarded as a movement from a condition of illegality to one of legality, but as a movement from a condition of legal *unspeakability* to one of legal *speakability*. My claim is that what matters in this context is the way in which LGB people have come to speak the legal language and to frame their concerns as users of the law. Eskridge is at pains to show that in the last decades the law has actually proved a more effective means of social change than statutory measures. His article intends to debunk the view that most often courts fail to produce significant social reform and that legal officials' hyper-activism can even be counter-productive as it tends to bring about 'backlash' from energized counter-movements. If this is the case, the transition that is affecting LGB rights campaigns can help capture what is involved in the passage from legal unspeakability to legal speakability and thus in the passage from a (mainly) political to a (mainly) legal shape of social struggles.

To explore this issue, Douglas NeJaime (2003) draws on Gary Bellow's (1996: 309) definition of *political lawyering* as a 'medium through which some of us with law training chose to respond to the need for change in an unjust world'. By doing so, NeJaime explores how legal experts engage in political struggles to effect socio-political change *through* law and how the means they use act back on the end they further. He points out that often lawyers find themselves constructing 'identities in order to achieve legal reform' (Bellow 1996: 519). While there is no doubt that the LGB community is by no means a sealed off, homogenous entity, but a polyvocal context where disagreeing visions of love, sex, relationships and kinship coexist and/or conflict, the need to lay claims to specific rights fosters the tendency to provide a unifying narrative. According to Yuvraj Joshi (2012) this narrative is modelled after the cultural unit pinpointed by Valverde, namely, the *monogamous couple based on love, fidelity and mutual commitment*, which confers 'respectability' on same-sex sexualities. Within this symbolic framework, a form of negotiation is taking place that leaves aside less acceptable aspects of same-sex sexuality and places emphasis on those that support a basic sameness between LGB and non-LGB individuals. Both NeJaime and Joshi trace this negotiation back to lawyers' need to couch convincing claims for their clients to be granted the rights attached to existing institutions, such as marriage, parenting and adoption. As Robert Leckey (2013: 7) observes with reference to lesbian parenting in Quebec, reference to the conventional lexicon of motherhood in order for it to cover the situation of a woman with no genetic ties to the child 'makes it likelier that she will be granted custody, an attribute of parental authority which is itself an effect of filiation'.

Based on this analysis, the shift from political to legal struggles reveals itself as a double movement eventuating in a change of the semiotic lexicon through which same-sex sexuality is cognized, recognized and self-recognized. On the one hand, in order to obtain social visibility *through* legal speakability, advocacy groups and lawyers frame the issue of recognition for same-sex sexuality in such a way that it may be converted into the existing legal lexicon. In this way, lesbians, gays and bisexuals are depicted as those who deserve a set of rights equal to different-sex people. Such a discursive strategy draws on the narratives of equality and sameness, whereby the unrecognition of the rights of lesbians, gays and bisexuals is not portrayed as the neglect of plural forms of sex and love, but as a *breach of the principles of the liberal state*. On the other hand, this strategy triggers a 'looping effect' (Hacking 1996; Sparti 2001), whereby the legal category that is produced to cover a given phenomenon acts back on those who use it to obtain rights. However strategic the purposes of a given category might be, its use on the part of the categorized subjects 'set[s] up distinctions by drawing boundaries and defining salience, hence producing cognitive constraints on the audience's identity-recognition span' (Sparti 2001: 344).

Against this background, it is worth looking at the historical trajectory of the shift I am touching upon. To this end, I would like to juxtapose two perceptive reconstructions of the shift in question. They cast light on different aspects and tease out different values attached to the new fashion of LGB rights battles. Eskridge (2013) and Diane Richardson (2000) reconsider the leap from the liberationism of the 1970s to present-day LGB rights struggles by advancing two typologies. Eskridge singles out three stages of political engagement and legal advocacy: *uphill struggles, politics of recognition* and *normal politics*. Richardson focuses on the types of claims that support rights battles in these stages (as far as the two typologies overlap): *conduct-based, identity-based* and *relationship-based* rights claims. Needless to say, these are generalizations that do not precisely correspond to distinct sequences of events that occurred in different geo-historical contexts. However, these two typologies help identify a key element of the trajectory at stake, that is to say, the connection between the change in LGB groups' strategy and the change in the type of narrative that underpins it.

Eskridge explains that initially (1970–1996) struggles for LGB rights, and for the recognition of same-sex relationships above all, were uphill because of a homophobic cultural background. LGB people could not procreate and were deemed to be unable to form serious relationships similar to marriage with children. This was generally the case until the traditional association of 'homosexuality' with sexual promiscuity slowly began to be replaced by association with family and commitment. In a second stage (1996–2008), advocacy groups and civil society organizations came to the conclusion that equality litigations need grass-roots mobilization and efforts to make political alliances. LGB movements needed to give life to a committed politics of recognition. In a later stage (post-2008), LGB issues became issues of normal politics focused on the consequences of different relationship-recognition regimes for different groups within society. The politics of same-sex sexuality became normal because the issue of gay and lesbian relationships came to be perceived as central to the bigger question of social utility as a whole and the further question of whether the legal recognition of lesbian and gay couples could be beneficial or detrimental to it. On Eskridge's reading, shifts and changes are bound up with precise historical events and landmark judicial rulings in the USA. Yet, as Richardson's analysis illustrates, such situation-specific events are instances of a broader transformation that has affected liberal states generally. Richardson's typology revolves around the type of claims that legal and political struggles voice. A relevant friction with Eskridge's view emerges as to the goal of LGB struggles. Indeed, Eskridge frames the issue of same-sex recognition in terms of recognition of same-sex relationships that, in his view, are perfectly comparable with different-sex ones. The recognition of lesbians, gays and bisexuals as being capable of engaging in committed and stable relationships, he believes, dispels a few misplaced anxieties about the alleged antisocial nature of homosexuality. This view hinges on Eskridge's conviction that gays and lesbians have always conceived of themselves as individuals apt to form couples. It follows that no major shift occurred in the self-perception of (at least the bulk of) the LGB community. In Richardson's more critical reading, on the contrary, there was something specifically different in LGB conceptions of love and sex before the later stages that Eskridge describes. The political strategies Eskridge accounts for were animated by different concerns than the need for recognition of intimate relationships.

Richardson believes *conduct-based rights* claims were typical of early stages of LGB struggles before the 1990s. She points out that, as these struggles centred on the admissibility of sexual acts, they did not pursue recognition of any specific form of sexual identity. They aimed at making sure that the law might grant the right for an adult, under certain specific contexts, to engage in sexual acts with another adult. This right can hardly identify anyone as bisexual, gay or lesbian. Moreover, the understanding of sexual practices underlying these claims exerted a disruptive power on mainstream heterosexual ones. A central element at stake was not just the mere right to engage in sexual acts, but the right to gratification of sexual desire. The narrative of reproduction, so central to different-sex sexual practice, was replaced by the right to individual pleasure as well as the recognition of women's sexual needs advocated by feminists.

A relevant change pinpointed by Richardson is the prominence attached to identity in the rights talk from the 1980s onwards. It became the spearhead of the new sexual battles when openly homosexual or pro-homosexual scientists started emphasizing the genetic connotation of both sexual difference and sexual orientation (Bleier 1984; Fausto-Sterling 1985, 2012; Keller 1995; Spanier 2005). Homosexuality came to be regarded as something inborn, unchosen and unchangeable – in short, 'something over which they have no control' (Spanier 2005: 33). From a nuanced understanding of identity as embedded in the flux of ongoing negotiations with available social categories and with one's social milieu (see, for example, Hammack and Cohler 2009), sexual identity ended up being associated with the presence of a 'gay gene' (see, for example, Hamer and Copeland 1994). Richardson insists on the relevance to rights claims of one's sexual identity not being chosen but affixed to nature. On the one hand, the rights discourse clung to the concept itself of citizenship, which in its turn entails a right to self-expression. If gayness is innate, LGB citizens can neither be asked to efface part of what they are nor be denied the rights and benefits associated with citizenship. On the other hand, however, such an objectified notion of identity altered the nature of LGB rights. While before they were focused on sexual pleasure and the legalization of once criminalized sexual conduct, subsequently LGB rights became a sub-species of minority rights: '[W]ithin the established boundaries of tolerance, a limited right to express one's identity as a tolerated "minority"' (Richardson 2000: 122; see also Herman 1990 and Cooper 2001).

Nevertheless, Richardson goes on to say, a more significant change affected the *context* where rights are supposed to be exercised. Same-sex rights became associated with a specific relational structure, that is, the couple. As Teemu Ruskola (2005: 239) comments in his dexterous analysis of the US Supreme Court decision *Lawrence v. Texas* (2003), 'one would think that homosexuals exist *only* in relationships, and that relationships are the *only* context in which homosexuals might conceivably engage in sex acts'. The epitome of the new (legally sponsored) link between same-sex sexuality and relationships is a juncture of the aforesaid decision, where the majority opinion states that 'when sexuality finds overt expression in intimate conduct with another person, the conduct can be but one element in a personal bond that is more enduring. The liberty protected by the Constitution allows homosexual persons the right to make this choice' (*Lawrence v. Texas*, Opinion of the Court, Oral Argument Transcript: 6). Expression of one's sexuality finds room in a fourfold context comprising relationship, coupledom, privateness and choice (on this wavelength, see also the analysis of *Obergefell v. Hodges* in Daum 2017).

I should like to stress that the movement I am discussing should be regarded not so much as a dispute over the advantages and disadvantages of same-sex marriage as a cultural shift that occurs within a broader societal transformation. In effect, it is hard – and perhaps pointless – to seek to determine whether marriage is being beneficial or detrimental to LGB individuals and groups. The famed exchange between Tom Stoddard (1989) and Paula Ettelbrick (1989) cannot yet be adjudicated (Stein 2009).

The intra-community debate is still underway and concerns issues of politics, identification and ideology, rather than strategy (Ball 2009). Stoddard espoused the approach of the civil rights movement and aimed to further the general project of obtaining equality for homosexuals. Marriage was a channel more than an end in itself. Ettelbrick was more sensitive to the reasons of erstwhile liberationist movements, who believed marriage to be part and parcel of a corrupted and decaying ideology imbued with sexism and heterosexism. Ettelbrick believed it is all the more necessary to change the way benefits and duties, typically associated with marriage, are distributed, and thus to devise alternatives to marriage.

As this pioneering exchange shows, the stake in the marriage debate is not the type or amount of benefits and rights that are likely (or unlikely) to be obtained, but the nature of same-sex political engagement. Those who merely focus on if and to what extent LGB people are likely to benefit from marriage or if and to what extent marriage depoliticizes same-sexual struggles risk talking past each other. On this account, as Jasbir Puar (2013: 24) puts it, we should not be concerned with legal instruments as such, but rather with 'the law's reliance on performative language that produces that which it simply claims to regulate, including the ascription of a subject of that law'. In this light, the transformation occurring in state family law and policy frameworks in many Western jurisdictions offers a glimpse into law's oblique performativity (see Introduction) and its interplay with what Schneider (1984) calls 'cultural units' behind kinship. Without a doubt, bridging the gap between actual sexual practices and legal texts empowers those who engage in once excluded forms of relationship. As Eskridge's typology points out, thanks to judicial pressure (and in some European cases legislative measures), the politics of sexual minorities exits the state of exception it has long occupied and enters the sphere of normal politics. In today's liberal states minority sexual groups have a say in the regulation of sexual conduct and intimate relationships. On the other hand, however, what mostly goes unnoticed is how people's recourse to law affects that which is not directly addressed by legal regulation. We should concern ourselves with how such an oblique regulation happens.

In my discussion above I wished to make the point that the core of the transition in question is the negotiation that is currently being conducted between the users of the law and the cultural units that they evoke in order to attain legal speakability. In other words, the linchpin of this societal process is the interplay between the natural fixity of reified cultural units and the mobilization of meaning that any attempt to change the former sparks. This problem was subtly captured, and boldly voiced, by Schneider (1997 – see Section 1.2) when he advanced the idea that social change unfolds along the lines drawn by cultural units. Much as he welcomed changes in the regulation of same-sex kinship, he articulated a few misgivings about these changes being able to disrupt mainstream understandings of kinship relations and their links with biology. Whether or not he was right on this particular issue – and this continues to be a moot point – Schneider makes it clear that change is always a 'bounded' change (see also Croce 2015a). Although socially available categories and institutions are challenged by the subjects who are excluded by a given social categorization, the latter (is claimed to) end up absorbing any potentially defiant use. Yet how come this process takes place? And in what ways does my emphasis on law-users help clarify it?

The frictions occurring in the interstices of the dominant kinship culture set in motion what Adam Green (2007) calls the 'performative interval'. This is a condition whereby the subject who (whether consciously or not) makes a subversive use of the dominant categorial grid remains trapped in the very linguistic repertoire that she aims to innovate. The performative interval illustrates how the individual who falls outside the dominant categorial grid 'acts towards' a symbolic formation – the role as is defined by that grid – and fills the gap between one's doing (the unnamed practice) and one's identity (the configuration that one's actions take vis-à-vis the description provided for them). In doing so, her actions acquire a specific meaning as soon as they are labelled in a specific way within the institutional framework to which the individual seeks to gain access in order to acquire legal speakability and socio-political visibility. In this reading, Green (2007: 32) forcefully insists on 'the irreducibility of the subject to a presocial or prelinguistic self' to underline that there is no neutral distance separating the act from its description. It is not the case that particular acts can be described in multiple ways: in performing an act described in such and such a way, the agent is assuming the identity that the institutional framework qualifies in such and such a way. The performative interval, therefore, serves as an intellectual device useful to show, at least from a heuristic viewpoint, how the intercourse between acts and identities (inscribed in roles) tends to turn any defiance of the official grid into a reaffirmation of it.

This account sheds a different light on the ongoing developments in the field of family law that I mentioned above, in particular those that are designed to extend the scope of the relationships that are granted the right to form a family (see also Section 1.3). Insofar as this extension unfolds as an extension of the 'already available', a process of 'normalization' that redresses defiant uses does not stem from any 'intentional' machinations of scheming political conservatives who want to expunge the abnormal. Such a top-down view finds no room in an interpretative framework centred on law-users. Rather, the interplay between legal kinship categories and social practices unfurls as *a two-way process of mutual constitution and legitimation* (see Swennen and Croce 2016). Minority sexual practices furnish the substantive contents for the law to issue new rules on family and kinship (binding formulations of official kinship relationships), whereas the law reinforces and legitimizes the former. In this way, two key functions of social interaction are performed. On the one hand, the flexibility and innate mutability of social practices is restrained by the solidifying and rigidifying force of legal provisions. On the other hand, the law can gain a stable foothold in the social realm by capitalizing on the normative resources and substantive contents deployed within social practices.

In short, the pursuit of socio-political visibility through legal speakability prompts marginalized sexual minorities to engage in an ongoing negotiation that achieves two goals. First, rights that have long been associated with the hegemonic culture are redistributed among a wider range of individuals. Second, former marginalized sexualities turn out to be included in the platform whose boundaries are marked by the official lexicon of legal kinship. This negotiation leads to an important transformation. Specific family law categories, such as 'marriage', 'wife', 'husband', 'family', 'parent' and 'child' continue to serve as descriptive devices for kinship roles, but the range of individuals who can perform these roles is broadened. Despite this, within such a bounded negotiation – 'bounded' because changes are conditional upon the acceptance of the hegemonic lexicon enshrined in law (see Croce 2015a) – the chances that this extension may serve as an effective form of resignification are slim. As soon as individuals act towards the symbolic formation of traditional roles, they are invested with the weighty load of the role's cognitive background and its narratives about exemplary models, good manners, general principles and widespread beliefs. The intercourse between one's performing a role in a potentially innovative way and the role's tendency to preserve its traditional shape would be likely to bring about effects only in the wake of the much broader societal process that Bourdieu (2001) describes as the neutralization of the unceasing activity of 'dehistoricization and externalization' of the structures that determine the sexist and heterosexist organization of society.

Based on the analysis so far, I would like to conclude this section by stressing the link between the developmental trajectories outlined by Eskridge and Richardson and the growing involvement of sexual minorities in the legal discourse. Former homosexual battles could obviously not hinge on the legal lexicon that was party to, and shored up, an oppressive sexual culture. With the demise of liberationist political engagement and the progressive spread of the rights discourse (see Venditti 2016), homosexual groups and their representatives adopted the strategy to gain access to society, rather than try to draw it to a close. This forced them to engage in a process of mutual translatability between the vocabulary that affected people use to make sense of, and account for, their experience, and the legal language, with its categories and formal structure. The concept of the looping effect and the notion of the performative interval have helped me pin down how the use of labels on the part of the subjects involved produces effects on their self-conceptualization and the way they give an account of themselves. In the light of that, charging legal developments themselves with being conducive to greater injustice is very problematic (nor, I believe, is this the point that queer and radical critics raise). Nevertheless, it is just as problematic to deny the remarkable change in the mainstream (straight and gay) vocabulary that articulates sexual life. It is up to a deeper analysis of political and socio-cultural phenomena to understand what lies beneath this change.

1.2 Remoulding kinship: subversion or assimilation?

One of the main conclusions of the previous section is that the ongoing revision of sexual categories is not necessarily characterized by an individualistic twist (see, for example, Eekelaar 2009: Chapter 1; Eekelaar 2012). Rather, the new scenario makes room for cultural units, such as the respectable couple, that serve to create spaces of (private) interaction freed from (public) shame. These are 'respectable' intimate contexts which are granted legal recognition and protection where previously censured sexualities may engage in publicly recognized patterns of interaction. As I explored, this process is conducive to new configurations of normality that tend to sterilize social conflicts and swell the rank of normal citizens. This is why some scholars claim that at present liberal states are more and more inclined to enter negotiations with new forms of sexuality to let them into patterns of ties that have so far been deemed to be exclusive property of the conventional family: national legal systems

> have begun to pay more attention to homosexual partnerships and alternative communities of cohabitation and caretaking beyond the conjugal nuclear family since former social welfare duties can be delegated to them as well. . . . Institutional recognition is bestowed, therefore, when it is of economic advantage to the state.
>
> (Woltersdorff 2011: 177)

In other words, it appears that the shrinking of the state and the parallel explosion of sexual pluralism collude in enlarging the existing grid of family forms.

On this reading, the state does not work as a repressive machinery, but achieves the lessening of social conflict by opening up spaces for constant negotiations with a view to normalizing rather than prohibiting. Accordingly, the increasing acceptance of formerly excluded sexual forms and kinship formations could be viewed as the flip-side of the gradual waning of traditional states and the infiltration of the neoliberal rationality. The question then is how and to what extent this process affects both parties, namely, citizens who call for recognition and the institutions that recognize. Is this negotiation, despite varying effects of normalization, likely to bring about a radical change in the traditional family grid (based on faithful, committed, long-lasting coupledom) and the conventional conception of kinship (based on blood ties and instrumental in reproduction)? If the effect of such a neoliberal 'sensitivity' to the plurality of life forms is a progressive one, can we look at this trajectory 'strategically' so as to interpret it as a beneficial fissure of disciplinary state apparatuses?

While, as I insisted, the disciplinary activity of governmental apparatuses is not the focus of this book, I think the questions mentioned above can be interpreted as contemporary instantiations of the more general social theory issue of the relationship between social practices and the context where they unfold. So, they deserve attention insofar as they have something significant to say about the scope and potential of the action of social agents. At its simplest, the question is whether the meaning of traditional social practices can vary, and, in doing so, trigger a change in the comprehensive context in which they are located. This question raises a dilemma that has taken many shapes in the history of social sciences. It can be summarized as follows: do practices, as basic constituents of social reality, acquire their specific meaning only within their socio-cultural context or does the socio-cultural context owe its meaning to the combination among its constituents? To put it bluntly, in the first case, practices would lose their meaning and become nonsensical should they challenge or escape the context; in the second case, the context would be dependent on its constituents and be sensitive to the changes they might undergo. To be sure, the context and its constituents are constantly involved in a process of mutual determination, and yet the issue to be tackled is their relative degree of autonomy from each other.

To take up this issue properly, and to see the shape it has taken in the areas of family law and the regulation of kinship, it is worth briefly tracing the history of the intellectual lens that is traditionally called 'kinship'. As I noted above, Schneider (1980; 1984) is the initiator of new kinship studies (see, for example, Collier and Yanagisako 1987; Carsten 2000; Franklin and McKinnon 2012), which parted ways with conventional approaches to this subject area in order to foreground the cultural, context-specific aspects of kinship as part and parcel of a society's symbolic universe. In truth, Schneider's seminal critique centred on kinship studies rather than kinship practices as such; or better, his influential view of kinship was conditional on his critique of kinship studies. Coming from the North American tradition of Lewis Morgan and Franz Boas, Schneider focused on the study of kinship terminology, which, in that tradition, was held to reveal the essence of kinship. Unlike his predecessors, though, Schneider's central concern was not with the structure or function of kinship, but with the production of social meanings that underpin kinship practices. In particular, he placed emphasis on potential frictions between the practical and the symbolic levels insofar as there is always a mismatch between the two. In short, Schneider set out to study kinship as a 'cultural unit'.

This view is based on a conception of social meanings, as well as their roles in social life, that is particularly alert to the constructedness of meaning and to the various forms of selection that underlie its production (see, for example, Croce 2015a). Schneider's argument reads as follows: if there is hardly anything natural in the way people construct practices and position them in their own biographies, the study of kinship has to draw on the ensemble of practices where kinship acquires specific significance as a cultural unit. Schneider deems cultural units to be interwoven intellectual artefacts that play a part in the complex conceptual tapestry through which social actors experience the world in a certain geo-historical context. The production of units implies 'sort[ing] certain elements out and keep[ing] others in, formulating from these elements a construct that can be communicated from one person to another, understood by both' (Schneider 1980: 4). This is the reason why units can never be exactly isomorphic with the entities they refer to. In this sense, cultural units are like words of ordinary language, which are not determined by their relation to their referent, but are immersed in a continuous interplay with other words in the practice of language. Schneider (1980: 4) avers that in order to capture the meaning of a word one needs to know 'which of the many meanings applies when, and which of the many meanings does not apply or is not relevant under what circumstances; and finally, how the different meanings of the word relate to each other'. Hence, what is crucial to the understanding of a unit is its relation to the other units in the cultural context where they are party to a broader symbolic universe as well as the numerous transformations they undergo while they are used in everyday life.

For my purposes, Schneider's methodological commitments are even more salient than his conclusions. He claims that one neglects the relevance of kinship if one thinks of it as an observable practice that is transparent to the observer's eye. No set of descriptions, however accurate they may be, can provide us with an exhaustive understanding of what kinship is. For it is a mobile and flexible intellectual utensil that people in a particular geo-historical context use to make sense of certain interactions in such and such a way. This is why, Schneider insists, kinship must be studied against the background of the complex canopy of practices where it is applied. In doing so, he exerted two main effects on the study of kinship. First, he relativized kinship, since he portrayed it as a key cultural means that allowed Euro-American culture to imagine the biological family as being at the core of every human collectivity. Second, he historicized kinship by turning it into an effective lens to look at the ways in which Western societies have been built upon a culture-specific configuration of kinship, pivoted on monogamous coupledom, biological ties and procreative sexuality.

A word on such two relevant effects. On the one hand, Schneider's analysis significantly scaled down the scope and claims of the study of kinship, as he laid bare the ethnocentric bias of traditional paradigms. Schneider (1984) pointed out that the way people practise, understand and talk about kinship should be part of its study, on top of the actual practice that the observer relates. This omission had led prior scholars, who founded and nurtured this subject area, to corroborate – whether wittingly or not – the Euro-American assumption that 'blood is thicker than water'. They straightforwardly mistook kinship and its strict rules for a human invariable, while, in reality, it is a culture-specific construct. According to Schneider (1984: 175), then, kinship studies before him were nothing but a convoluted variation on 'the ethnoepistemology of European culture'. On the other hand, he remarkably heightened the interdisciplinary fertility of kinship studies. Indeed, one of Schneider's main teachings is that the study of kinship serves as a tool for understanding the interrelationship between kinship and other domains, precisely because, as a cultural unit, kinship never coincides with the set of observable behaviours publicly displayed in daily interaction. Being comprehensible only in the light of their relation to other units and the way they are applied and reapplied in actual practice, 'the meanings attributed to the relations and actions of kin are drawn from a range of cultural domains, including religion, nationality, gender, ethnicity, social class, and the concept of "person"' (Collier and Yanagisako 1987: 6).

In the wake of Schneider's compelling critique, a number of authors in the field of cultural and social anthropology seized on the revitalization of kinship to explore new research directions. A milestone in this framework is Janet Carsten's (2000) edited book *Cultures of Relatedness*, which builds on ethnographic cases to support Schneider's intuition that kinship depends upon the place it occupies in the broader set of cultural units. The book's main contribution is to show that kinship practices in non-Western cultures are not based on biological reproduction. At the same time, Carsten's suggestion is that the semantic scope of kinship is limited and that it should be reformulated more broadly as 'relatedness'. On this reading, relatedness comes across as a term that best accounts for kinship as a way of addressing 'fundamental forms of human dependency, which may include birth, child rearing, relations of emotional dependency and support, generational ties, illness, dying, and death (to name a few)' (Butler 2004: 103). Building on this image of kinship as a wide set of relations, scholars in the field of new kinship studies seek to show that the boundaries between the biological and the social, which were the centrepiece of traditional studies on kinship, in many geo-historical contexts are blurred, if not absent completely. It is in this spirit that, in Carsten's book, Helen Lambert's analysis of kinship in north India, Barbara Bodenhorn's investigation into the Inupiat of northern Alaska, and Karen Middleton's analysis of the Karembola of Madagascar foreground the non-procreative foundations of kinship as well as kinship practices based on choice and agency.

I would like to leave here the trajectories of new kinship studies to focus on their relevance to the theme that opened this section, that is, the relationship between new conceptions of kinship and current transitions in law and politics. In particular, the transformative potentials of people trying to build on, and by doing so to revise, hegemonic practices. An appropriate entry point to this issue is a polemic exchange between Schneider (1997) and Corinne Hayden (1995). The subject of controversy was the development of assisted reproductive technologies (ART), which appears to be widening the rift between procreation and the nuclear family as its natural locus (Edwards et al. 1999). Specifically, ART is believed to be able to prompt a *renegotiation of the 'naturalness'* of family and parenthood and to make room for multiple parental figures, such as *genetic, birth, intentional* and *social* parents, no matter whether hetero-, homo-, bi- or trans-sexual. This push for the technologization of kinship shows that biological ties are being revisited and supplemented with other types of ties, centred on the spouses' individual choice (Weston 1991). ART puts individuals in the position to make decisions about procreation within a growing range of possibilities in many respects (Soini et al 2006). Consequently, as these techniques develop and are made available, another pillar of the conventional family – parenting – is being brought into question. With the help of ART, non-reproductive relationships are defying conventional grids of parent–children ties to the extent that, at present, a growing number of families is no longer constructed around the binary husband/wife, but is extended to social networks and lines of solidarity and friendship, within which parental responsibilities and entitlements are redistributed among a multiplicity of actors (see, for example, Dempsey 2010).

In the wake of these changes, a main conundrum surfaces, particularly whether or not the interaction between new phenomena concerning relatedness and available cultural units is likely to bring about a revision of the latter. Hayden (1995) builds on a vibrant literature (e.g. Weston 1991; Strathern 1992a; Ragoné 1994) that in the early 1990s was giving the lie to views that tied kinship to heterosexuality and natural procreation. In particular, she takes stock of Weston's dismissal of the conventional view which excluded familial ties between persons of the same sex because they were not grounded in biology or procreation and thus did not fit any tidy kinship division. Given that ART allows homosexuals to construct biological relationships, this unsettles the traditional criteria to establish what counts as kinship. In this way, not only do same-sex families challenge heterosexual kinship by shifting the emphasis *from blood to choice*, they also cast light on the *constructedness* of the latter. Drawing from an analysis of lesbians who create families through donor insemination and thus make biology both explicit and mutable, Hayden (1995: 54) puts forward a 'kinetic reading of generation, of bringing into being', which 'supersedes genetic connection as the privileged signifier of relatedness'.

In a short, controversial article on the literature on LGB families and alternative routes to creating family ties, Schneider (1997) offers what could be called a 'culturalist' interpretation of these phenomena. Building on an idea of cultural systems as dominant ideologies, where culture plays out as a hegemonic discourse, he claims that LGB people who construct families

> do these things because they live in this society and are steeped in this culture, as everyone is. And like everyone else who is human, they want to do what they are supposed to do, they want to feel what they are supposed to feel, they want to believe what they are supposed to believe, and have the rewarding and fulfilling life that they were explicitly and implicitly promised as they grew up.
>
> (Schneider 1997: 271)

He substantiates his argument by depicting everyday language, and especially kinship terms, as a frame of significance with axiological and pragmatic bearings insofar as they attribute both values and roles: '[G]ays and lesbians will use the term *cousin* for the children of their mothers' and fathers' brothers, and the terms *nephew* and *niece* for their siblings' children' (Schneider 1997: 271). In other words, Schneider downplays the subversive force of same-sex kinship because he claims it reflects previous distinctions and classifications of conventional kinship.

More recently, socio-legal scholars have offered a similar argument, especially when it comes to homosexuals' family members asking for legal recognition. Alison Diduck (2007) analyzes how same-sex parents struggle to be socially perceived as 'real' families and to have their relationships perceived as 'normal'. Whether or not this process is likely to revolutionize the conventional 'natural' family, legal regulation still clings to a form of biological determinism in its pursuit of a 'genetic "truth"' that links 'it to both welfare and rights' (Diduck 2007: 468). On this account, whether or not same-sex families are being accepted as 'real' families, the matrix that is being used to grant recognition is one that places value on kinship based upon genetics precisely because non-heterosexual families are being legitimized by being presented as based on biology. Diduck points out that this has mainly to do with what, with reference to Hester Lessard (2004), she calls 'context-stripping', which subtly captures the conundrum I am toying with. On the one hand, the open-ended language of formal equality and the use of seemingly neutral concepts such as 'parent, spouse, best interests of the child, and family provide opportunity for progressive interpretations that enlarge the scope of social inclusion' (Lessard 2004: 207). On the other hand, the socio-cultural as well as the institutional contexts 'place significant limits on what meanings are likely to find acceptance' (Lessard 2004: 207).

In the framework of this more recent critique, Schneider's sceptical account seems to find support in the analysis of those recognition strategies that I discussed in the previous section. To be more accurate, Schneider's account is both amended and reinforced. In fact, it is not the mere force of one's culture that instructs one in where to place one's practices as well as in the value one has to attach to them. Schneider's conception of culture as a hegemonic set of signs that draws the borders of people's imagination is too static and deterministic. Studies on how new legal categories are produced that accommodate same-sex kin formations lay emphasis on the active role of people's use of the legal instruments providing for recognition and protection. Put otherwise, as I argued in Section 1.1, it is the way people use categories (above all with a view to attaining legal effects) that impacts on the scope and nature of the cultural unit of kinship. The notion of context-stripping illustrates how different manifestations of kinship are treated as though they were alike in order for excluded forms of relationships and parenting to be granted the protection offered to non-excluded ones. As Diduck (2007) notes, this produces inadvertent but detrimental outcomes. First, the historical disadvantages of same-sex kinship formations – not only those related to sexual orientation (see Section 1.3) – are concealed and depoliticized. Second, different types of kinship practices that occur in same-sex and different-sex kinship formations are homogenized by a new normative idealization of the family, which paradoxically ends up reinstating the preeminence of biology.

This all seems to attest to the paradoxical condition whereby the moment biology loses its 'status of a prior fact' (Strathern 1992b: 194), it becomes more evident. Charis Cussins Thompson's (Cussins 1998; Thompson 2001) studies on infertility clinics foreground how patients, practitioners, third-party donors, medical techniques, and regulatory standards partake in coordinated processes of naturalization and normalization. To different degrees, they all contribute to making ART reproduce 'legitimate and intact chains of descent' (Thompson 2001: 175) by elaborating certain aspects and omitting others. The examples she discusses showcase people's ability to manipulate and rework the fine line separating nature from culture in such a way that the 'nature' of biology is preserved exactly through a cultural process of joint, multi-party elaboration. It is then in this ambivalent remaking of the spheres of biology and culture that genetic bonds make their comeback as the device that assures the sameness of kinship models. As Sarah Franklin maintains in her enlightening study of in-vitro fertilization (IVF), ART

> reproduce, and condense, familiar narratives – from the naturalness of reproduction and the universal desire for parenthood to the value of scientific progress and the benefits of medical assistance – and the success of IVF is in turn offered as proof, or evidence, of how these logics fit together.
>
> (Franklin 2013: 6)

Based on the analysis above, can the controversy between Schneider and Hayden be adjudicated? And how could this help us answer the question of the alleged collusion between neoliberalism and sexual pluralism? The preceding section has already foregrounded the key role of the users of the law in the production and reproduction of the cultural units that they have recourse to when they demand legal speakability. My reading avoids culturalist pitfalls and at the same time offers a realistic account of the way changes of the constituents in a context always stem from a negotiation between the two, as looping effects and the performative interval oversee the 'accommodation' of emerging practices in the 'already available' stock of dominant practices. In that respect, the critical analysis of the authors mentioned above casts an ambivalent light on the new trajectories of new kinship formations, whether different- or same-sex. But exactly because of this ambivalence, the hegemonic force of the context should not be mistaken for an inescapable fate if it is the case, as I believe it is, that a crucial variable in the production of counter-hegemonic meanings is the way in which people understand their relationships (be these sexual or emotional ones) and the political role they attribute to their own being 'at the margins'. While the previous section focused on the erasure of difference that is (involuntarily) engendered by LGB relationships' movement from legal unspeakability to legal speakability, there are ways of making difference matter that place value on what exceeds the frame of significance marked out by cultural units and is left aside by normalization. An illustrative example is the way of conceiving the phenomenon of *polyamory*, which involves adults in multiple-partner emotional and/or sexual relationships (Klesse 2007; Barker and Langdridge 2010; Sheff 2011). While a thorough analysis of this phenomenon would deserve a book of its own, my more limited intention here is to consider it as an example of practices that claim to preserve their defiant attitude towards normalized sexual lifestyles.

On the one hand, polyamory has been criticized by some authors because it is founded on apolitical motivations (Wilkinson 2010) or because it inadvertently reproduces typical dynamics of monogamy as an organizing and authenticating principle (Finn and Malson 2008). In this regard, polyamory seems to follow in the footsteps of other forms of queer kinship that emerged as alternative but eventually failed to escape the disciplinary effects of normalization. On the other hand, there are authors who resist this slippery slope and insist on polyamory being a position more than a sexual lifestyle – one that calls into action with an eye to creating awareness on those conditions that favour processes of normative construction and dehistoricization of patterns of relationship like monogamy. In this latter sense, polyamory is not tantamount to indulging in a sexual behaviour that accommodates one's exotic sexual fantasies. It is at one and the same time a form of symbolic resistance and an instance of political commitment to pluralism broadly speaking.

In 2006, a special issue of the journal *Sexualities* was devoted to teasing out the political significance of polyamory vis-à-vis the multiple forms of naturalization and normalization of kinship I have discussed so far. The issue editors invite us to understand polyamory, and non-monogamy more generally, as conducive to 'novel insights into the social construction and organization of kinship, households and the family, parenting practices, sexual identities and heteronormativity' (Haritaworn et al. 2006: 518). While polyamory is generally dismissed as debauchery and antisocial pleasure both in public culture and in judicial settings (see, for example, Emens 2004), in their engaging introduction the issue editors reclaim the legacy of liberationist movements (see, for example, Red Collective, [1973]1978; Gay Liberation Front, [1973]1978), insofar as they viewed monogamy as a compulsory ideal (see also Robinson 1997). These movements held the view that, when replicated by LGB people, monogamy is inevitably 'a parody' that feeds a model of relationship based 'on ownership – the woman sells her services to the man in return for security for herself and her children – and is entirely bound up in the man's idea of property' (Gay Liberation Front, [1973]1978). The Gay Liberation Front lamented the permeation of the emotional dishonesty of staying in the comfy safety of the home and garden, the security and narrowness of the life built for two, with the secret guilt of fancying someone else while remaining in thrall to the idea that true love lasts a lifetime – as though there were a ration of relationships, and to want more than one were greedy.

(Gay Liberation Front [1973]1978)

Haritaworn and colleagues (2006: 518) claim polyamory has arisen precisely from such emancipatory discourses and hence 'tries to provide languages and ethical guidelines for alternative lifestyles and sexual and intimate relationships beyond the culture of "compulsory monogamy"'.

This understanding of polyamory as a potentially subversive kinship practice helps provide a tentative answer to the question that commenced this section. Polyamory involves an attempt at tracing the history of the loving couple as a cultural unit that has almost entirely absorbed kinship and has made it collapse into the monogamous family. This is a genuinely political form of engagement for three main reasons. First, it is not merely deconstructive and critical, but constructive and practical in the first place. Poly communities are invited to stay open to 'those whose intimacies are most in need of emancipation – those whose bodies and sexualities have been violently exploited, demonized and suppressed through racism, transphobia, ablism and other systems of oppression' (Haritaworn 2006: 523). Second, this openness rests on polyamory escaping the fixity of sexual orientation (Klesse 2014) to further a more flexible idea of intimate practices bound up with mutable sexual identity, exposed to the flow of constant negotiations. If this reflects more faithfully the condition of non-monogamous bisexuals (Robinson 2013), the political significance of this position is much more generally the disposal of rigid binaries that 'obstruct the intelligibility of intersex, transgender, gender-queer or pan-gender identities and erotic subjectivities' (Klesse 2014: 95). Third, at the more fundamental level of social meaning, polyamory is an attempt to construct a language of sex, love, intimacy and affection that circumvents symbolic constraints and allows thinking of experiences that divert from conventional ones (Ritchie and Barker 2006). In this respect, the practice of polyamory challenges the limits of the frame of significance where monogamy represents both a legitimizing and an epistemological device and thus erodes its normative pre-eminence through reworking those language categories upon which the basic experiences of sex and love are founded.

The potential link between small-scale defiance and social change makes this latter type of pluralism appear less appealing to neoliberal policies, which tend to lessen social conflict and to foster plurality through the commodifying logic of the market. The active role and political awareness of the subjects involved turns out to be the element that drives changes in one direction or another: the refusal to perform context-stripping is as costly from the point of view of legal recognition as it is rewarding from the point of view of one's deliberate identification of the main features of the practice in which one is involved. This does not necessarily mean rejecting legal recognition, but forcing the law to revise the canons through which it recognizes (Swennen and Croce 2016; Swennen and Croce 2017), and in particular to pay more heed to the production of both new meanings and new patterns of conduct in people's daily practices. This is hardly mere recognition of what exists in the social realm, but an acceptance of the infinite plurality of social life and the connected risk that practices might clash and conflict. This is something to which this book will return (see Chapter 2, Section 2.2, and Conclusion). Before doing so, it is worth exploring how the law at times hampers the construction of new patterns and practices as it exerts its exclusive power to decide on the boundaries of the natural and the normal.

1.3 Filtering social practices

There is little doubt that the issues and the debates I have so far discussed revolve around the institution of the family as a pillar of Euro-American societies. As such, it is enshrined in the legal systems of contemporary liberal states, protected (in some cases) by constitutional provisions and governed by family law. And yet, the regulation of family is perhaps the branch of law where the constructedness of legal categories emerges with striking self-evidence. In his sociology of the juridical field, Bourdieu (1987: 846) contends family law is the area where the legal system deploys 'a whole arsenal of institutions and constraints' to protect the transmutation it performs of 'regularity (that which is done regularly) into rule (that which must be done), factual normalcy into legal normalcy'. By virtue of this artificial mechanism, says Bourdieu (1987: 847), family law contributes to 'the imposition of a representation of normalcy according to which *different* practices tend to appear *deviant*, anomalous, indeed abnormal, and pathological' and hence ratifies and validates 'as "universal" norms family practices that developed slowly, propelled by the efforts of the dominant class's moral avant garde'.

It is no coincidence that feminist theorists associated women's symbolic and material subjugation with the capitalist family (see, for example, Barrett and McIntosh 1982; Smart 1984). In the same critical vein, lesbian theorists encouraged revolt against an institution that fosters men's right to own women and to submit them to an unpaid labour system of housework and childcare (see, for example, Bunch 1987; Wittig 1992). Despite these ferocious attacks, however, people's and states' attitudes towards the family appear to have followed the trajectory I have sketched in the foregoing sections. In today's Western legal systems, the notions of family and family life (although revisited in some essential elements, as we have illustrated) serve as an effective mechanism of inclusion and recognition. This change is reflected in (some) feminists' reconceptualization of the family as

> the symbol of that last area where one has any hope of individual control over one's destiny, of meeting one's basic human needs, of nourishing that core of personhood threatened by vast impersonal institutions and uncontrollable corporate and government bureaucracies.
>
> (Friedan 1998: 218)

At the same time, as Didi Herman (1990: 797) warned as early as 1990, lesbian relationships are well on the way to espousing a notion of family that 'necessitates the productive, reproductive, and sexual exploitation of women by men', bound up with a notion of marriage as 'the legal tie binding women to family'. Herman (1990: 797) concludes that '[b]y appropriating familial ideology, lesbians and gay men may be supporting the very institutional structures that create and perpetuate women's oppression' and that lesbians'

> reliance on the language of monogamy, cohabitation, life-long commitment, and other essentials of *bona fide* heterosexual coupledom may divide us, not only from other lesbians and gays who do not live in this fashion, but from all people defined as 'single' by virtue of their exclusion from the model.
>
> (Herman 1990: 797)

In short, despite the ongoing and largely successful process of 'démariage' (Théry 1993), whereby marriage turns from the public performance of a civic ritual into the governance of private matters; despite the decrease in marriage's sway on how individuals organize and plan their intimate lives (Eekelaar 2009); despite the *nuclear* family gradually becoming *unclear* (Simpson 1998) because of changes that have irreversibly altered contemporary family formations; despite all this, the family as a key institution of contemporary societies still figures as an indispensable legal device if it is true, as it is, that many personal relationships, whether different- or same-sex, still need 'to be characterized as "family" for the purpose of the relevant legislation' (Eekelaar 2009: 31).

One might wonder why the legacy of past critiques of family and family law did not affect the force of such an institution as a legitimacy-conferring device. Or why the deep alterations just mentioned were not able to topple the family as the key domain of (publicly recognized) private life. If some anthropologists think this provides the grounds for holding that feminist, queer and radical 'rethinkings' of family are going too far in denying the monogamous family being a universal feature of human kinship (see, for example, Shapiro 2012), others contend that, on the contrary, critiques of family did not cut deep enough. This is what Will Kymlicka (1991) avers in his extensive review of Susan Moller Okin's *Justice, Gender, and the Family* (1989).

Kymlicka's analysis sheds light on both a few incongruities and the crypto-naturalistic assumptions of positions that claim to pose a threat to the deep-seated sexist structure of political institutions. In her influential book, Okin contends that the dominant conception of sexual inequality and the state policies meant to eliminate the imbalances this inequality brings about are poorly equipped for redressing substantial disparities between the sexes. In particular, they fail to identify the root cause of sexual inequality, that is, the basic organization of the family. For Okin, the rhetoric concerning women's instinctual proclivity for the care of the progeny and their scarce involvement in the political domain have to do with the alleged naturalness of motherhood as well as with the confinement of family dynamics to the private domain (understood as 'the other' with respect to the public/political one). In this reading, the double effect of naturalization and confinement is conducive to the systematic concealment of the practices that give rise to gender differences.

Whereas Kymlicka mostly agrees with this diagnosis, he has some misgivings about the prognosis and the cure. Okin submits that the short-term solution is the protection of vulnerable individuals, while the long-term one requires the construction of a society thoroughly indifferent to gender differences, one where sex plays no part in the allocation of rights, obligations, resources and responsibilities. In this type of society, the presumed naturalness of sex roles would not impinge on the care of children and domestic labour. Rather, there would be an equal sharing by men and women of paid and unpaid work. Kymlicka casts some doubts on this perspective: is it really true that it paves the way for a deep rethinking of the sexist matrix of society? Is it really true that recipes *à la* Okin help undo the naturalization of a human artefact and the normative value attached to it? In order to show that Okin does not make her case, Kymlicka (1991: 83) raises a much deeper and certainly more disquieting question: 'Who has the right to form a family?'

Kymlicka demonstrates that Okin's perspective is still affected by exclusionary prejudices. In the end, she holds on to a conventional notion of family and oscillates between a dehistoricizing conservatism (when she treats the typical Western family formation as the family *par excellence*) and a radical progressivism (when she advocates revision of the rhetoric of the natural family and the natural allocation of sexual labour). In this way, the key to women's liberation is believed to be the redistribution of domestic labour. But it ends there. This is why Kymlicka advances the hypothesis that a more effective revision of the conventional family might need a punchier approach to the Euro-American model of family with an eye to bringing to the surface the broader range of excluded and vulnerable subjects whose kin practices and structures are put on the margins of respectable Western societies, such as polygamous family assemblages.

I would like to take Kymlicka's challenge seriously and to look at the process that expelled the question of who has the right to form a family from the Western political imagination. One of the forms in which the naturalization of kinship relations manifests itself is precisely the removal of this question from the horizon of Western political and legal theorizing. In this regard, it is important to remark that, *pace* Okin (1989: 122; emphasis in original), the organization of family she excoriates is by no means 'a peculiarly *pre*liberal anomaly in modern society'. The meticulous regulation of family dynamics on the part of the state as well as their confinement to the private domain do not date back very far. Indeed, it is as young as liberalism.

In her thoughtful inquiry into the issue of whether marriage is status or contract, Janet Halley (2011a, 2011b) shows that it was the final accomplishment of national states in the 19th century, along with the creation of the brand-new branch of family law, which subtracted marriage from the general process of liberalization of society. More radically, both in the USA and Europe, the state turned marriage into a non-contractual institution in order to gain the upper hand on the regulation of family dynamics. Halley illustrates how the naturalization of family relationships went hand in hand with the internal movements of the capitalist society that intended to bolster the autonomy of sub-state sectors. Paradoxically, the progressive contractualization of the latter furthered the transformation of family into a uniform institution and the relationships among its members into specific status positions. In effect, Halley (2011a: 7) explains, 19th-century state law was not only intent on producing individuals with 'general rights'. In fact, in law branches like family law, the state was committed to the production of 'distinct "persons" with highly particular social beings'. In other words, under the guise of a liberal legal framework orchestrating the interactions of private individuals, modern legal systems aimed to enshrine in the law exemplary models and specific institutional figures – while those figures were meant to reflect and foster the models and figures developed within the institutions that the state recognized and promoted.

As far as the family is concerned, the way to its complete institutionalization was the regulation of marriage as a public ritual conveying a message of mutual fidelity and life-long commitment between two individuals who desire to change their status through it. Halley's investigation provides evidence that the new family law was meant to treat marriage not in terms of a mere contract between individual parties, but as a civil institution, 'the most interesting and important in its nature of any in society' (Joseph Story quoted in Halley 2011a: 19). Such a metamorphosis is astonishing. In the legal frameworks typical of the *Ancien Régime*, the regulation of family was based on disjointed bundles of legal provisions that governed distinct family relationships, such as the husband to the wife, or the father to the children and the other members of the family at large (mostly the servants). The 'household' was a complex and multi-layered microcosm comprised of parallel and fuzzily interconnected legal relationships, where the father's role was akin to a custodian's or a master's. For example, Halley (2011a: 2) argues, also the top of the pyramid, the father, was 'not one but three legal persons. The wife, the child, and the servant were not just subordinate; they were similarly subordinate'. Quite the reverse, modern family law turned the family into a homogenous, nuclear and compact cell, with a set number of institutional figures, whose boundaries were regulated by a limited and unitary range of legal provisions. The parties of such a foundational unit of society could hardly be conceived as autonomous wills bound together by contract, but as naturally connoted institutional figures whose union was performatively brought into existence by a public ritual. At the same time, these legal developments were fuelled by what Halley (2011a: 3) defines as an 'ideology', whereby 'the husband, wife, and child . . . lived in an affective, sentimental, altruistic, ascriptive, and morally saturated legal and social space' (on the 'ideology' of family see also Andersen 1991 and Collins 2001).

This historically nuanced understanding of the family and the pivotal role its conventional image still plays at present (see, for example, Pilecki and Hammack 2015) provide the key to decoding the main point raised by the various critical voices examined in the previous sections of this chapter. It should be clear by now that, by and large, they concur that political and legal progressions are hallmarked by a tendency to subsume formerly excluded sexualities and kinship practices under a conventional and normalizing understanding of family and family life, still tightly anchored to a conventional constellation of values. As a consequence, if inevitably some important traits of the latter are doomed to be altered, the final upshot is likely to be a reworked range of respectable sexualities and a renewed grid of legitimate kinship. As I sought to document above, this slippery slope is likely to engender two consequences. On the one hand, the subversive potential of formerly stigmatized sexualities could be sacrificed for the acquisition of a bundle of rights that are still conditional upon set forms of state-supported unions. On the other hand, the recognition of some sexual minorities could be instrumental in excluding (with indirect legal effects but direct symbolic outcomes) potentially more dangerous challenges raised by kinship formations that thoroughly fail to come to terms with the values of the conventional family.

To conclude this chapter with the discussion of a telling example, I would like to offer a glimpse into the way the law oversees the boundaries between admissible and non-admissible forms of relationships by focusing on a recent decision of the European Court of Human Rights (ECtHR), where the sitting judges had to face a remarkably challenging defiance of the traditional kinship grid. In *Burden and Burden v. the United Kingdom* (2008) two elderly sisters, who had lived together in a stable, committed and mutually supportive relationship all their lives, wanted to be exempted from paying the inheritance tax when one of the two would die. The two sisters complained under Article 14 of the European Convention on Human Rights taken in conjunction with Article 1 of Protocol No. 1 that, when the first of them died, the survivor would be required to pay inheritance tax on the dead sister's share of the family home, whereas the survivor of a married couple or a homosexual relationship registered under the UK Civil Partnership Act 2004 would be exempt from paying inheritance tax in these circumstances. Therefore, they claimed they should be recognized as a couple under the Civil Partnership Act. This act establishes that a couple is eligible to form a civil partnership if they are (i) of the same sex; (ii) not already married or in a civil partnership; (iii) over the age of 16; and (iv) not within the prohibited degrees of relationship.

The application was initially allocated to a Chamber within the Fourth Section of the ECtHR. The Chamber's conclusion is of high significance. The sitting judges found that there was no violation of Article 14 because the difference of treatment for the purposes of the grant of social security benefits was justified on the grounds that marriage was an institution 'widely accepted as conferring a particular status on those who entered it' (*Burden and Burden v. the UK* 2008: § 47). Moreover, the justices reasoned, the UK government's submission was to be accepted because the inheritance tax exemption for some married and civil partnership couples 'pursued a legitimate aim, namely to *promote stable, committed heterosexual and homosexual relationships* by providing the survivor with a measure of financial security after the death of the spouse or partner' (*Burden and Burden v. the UK* 2008: § 47; emphasis added). In other words, the decision seems to suggest, it is the discretionary power of the state that provides the grounds for rejecting the analogy between a partnership and the stable relationship of two siblings. The judgment unabashedly brings to light the selective power of state policies: it is for political institutions to determine who belongs to the range of citizens who are endowed with some rights and benefits, which in turn are meant to promote certain family formations to the disadvantage of others. Accordingly, the state cannot 'be criticised for pursuing, through its taxation system, policies designed to promote marriage; nor can it be criticised for making available the fiscal advantages attendant on marriage to committed homosexual couples' (*Burden and Burden v. the UK* 2008: § 47). In other words, by policy measures, the state has the right to shape the social domain in accordance with well-defined ideals and models of family.

Pursuant to a request by the applicants, the panel of the Grand Chamber decided to refer the case to the Grand Chamber. The sitting judges agreed with the former judgment that there was no violation of Article 14, but for surprisingly different reasons.

It is important to notice that the UK government's submission insisted on marriage and Civil Partnership Act unions being forbidden to close family members. The bare fact that the Burdens have decided to live together all their adult lives, as do many married and Civil Partnership Act couples, did not alter what the representative of the government defined as an essential difference between the two types of relationship. The main line of reasoning advanced by the representative of the UK government to discredit the applicants' claim appears relevant for this book's purposes. The Burdens could not claim to be in an analogous situation to a couple created by marriage or civil partnership, since the '*very essence of their relationship was different*' (*Burden and Burden v. the UK* 2008: § 49; emphasis added). What type of essence did the representative of the government have in mind? In truth, he did not refer to the essence of the social practices that legal provisions aimed to regulate. Instead, he referred to *the essence established by the law for legal purposes*. The representative of the government pointed out that 'a married or Civil Partnership Act couple chose to become connected by a formal relationship, recognised by law, with a number of legal consequences; whereas for sisters, the relationship was an accident of birth' (*Burden and Burden v. the UK* 2008: § 49). In addition, he continued to say, the relationship between siblings is indissoluble, whereas that between married couples and civil partners can be broken.

On their part, the applicants insisted that they could properly be regarded as being in a similar situation to a married or same-sex Civil Partnership Act couple. In fact, while it was true that many siblings are connected by nothing more than their common parentage, this was far from being the case with the Burden sisters, who

> had chosen to live together in a loving, committed and stable relationship for several decades, sharing their only home, to the exclusion of other partners. Their actions in so doing were just as much an expression of their respective self-determination and personal development as would have been the case had they been joined by marriage or a civil partnership.
>
> (*Burden and Burden v. the UK* 2008: § 53)

However, no matter how hard the applicants tried to couch the issue in keeping with the prevailing narrative of coupledom – where commitment, fidelity and respect appear to override sexual intercourse – their attempt turned out to be unsuccessful.

The opinion of the Grand Chamber is a genuine exercise in social ontology, aimed at penetrating the essence of relationships. At the same time, however, it betrays constructionist nuances as it refers to the way relationships are defined by the law. The naturalist and the constructionist bodies of the sentence short-circuit and give life to a stunning concealment of the core of the issue, that is, the selection of practices by state authorities. The majority opinion commences by remarking that the relationship between siblings 'is qualitatively of a different nature to that between married couples and homosexual civil partners under the United Kingdom's Civil Partnership Act' (*Burden and Burden v. the UK* 2008: § 63). The sitting judges basically claimed that the true *essence* of the connection between siblings is consanguinity, which under UK law was listed as an impediment to both partnership and marriage. Evidently, the justices took a leap from the level of nature to the juridical level, hidden behind the diaphanous veil of the typical circularities of the legal language. The two sisters were claiming that the law's choice to look at a natural trait as an impediment failed to do justice to their life-long choice to live together. Albeit the sisters were clearly moved by self-interested motives, they wanted to denounce the arbitrary violence of the law that promotes a natural fact to an unquestionable reason for exclusion.

At one juncture, the Grand Chamber seemed to revert to a more realist perspective. The majority opinion acknowledges that a state is legitimated to distinguish some unions from others so as to confer a special status on the former: people who desire to take advantage of these policy measures have to make their mutual commitment known to the whole society via public rituals performed under the eyes of state authorities or their representatives. Only in this case, the majority opined, can the length and the contents of a given relationship be considered as relevant variables. And yet, the judgment got caught again in a vicious circle. On one side, what gives life to a legitimate relationship is the public commitment before the law. On the other, this path is legally precluded to siblings. How then could this line of reasoning be relevant to the issue at stake?

All in all, the Grand Chamber's chief intention seemed to circumvent the bumpy road taken by the Chamber a few years before in December 2006. It was much safer to embark on an inquiry into the essence of relationships than bluntly recognize the state's right to exclude through policy measures. This is precisely what a few separate opinions bemoaned. Justice Nicolas Bratza voiced his disappointment by straightforwardly saying that the majority actually ducked the core of the issue. The majority opinion had omitted to tackle the question (raised by the Chamber of the Fourth Section) of the right of state policies to promote some models of relationships and family formations at the expense of others. However, Justice David Thór Björgvinsson did not mince words. In his concurring opinion he declared the reasoning of the majority to be flawed as it was founded on the argument that consanguinity between the Burdens prohibited them from entering into a legally binding agreement similar to marriage or civil partnership. He maintained that in principle nothing prevents the relationship between the sisters from being compared to married or civil partnership couples. Rather he continued to say the difference in treatment was objectively and reasonably justified because 'the institution of marriage is closely linked to the idea of the family, consisting of a man and a woman and their children, as one of the cornerstones of the social structure in the United Kingdom, as well as in the other member States of the Council of Europe' (Judge Björgvinsson's concurring opinion in *Burden and Burden v. the UK* 2008). Judge Boštjan Zupančič's dissenting opinion used logics to demonstrate that 'making consanguinity an impediment is simply arbitrary' (Judge Zupančič's dissenting opinion in *Burden and Burden v. the UK* 2008). Finally, in a further dissenting opinion, Justice Javier Borrego Borrego contended that the Grand Chamber had neglected to provide a convincing justification for the real issue at stake – the difference in treatment for tax purposes – and had taken refuge in a mere description of the facts with reference to consanguinity and its legal consequences.

In the end, whether or not they denied there was a violation of Article 14 of the European Convention on Human Rights, what all separate opinions emphasized was that the majority opinion had intentionally avoided facing the bare issue and had resorted to a convoluted strategy pivoted on the alleged nature of relationships. In one way or another, they all pointed out that what was really at stake was the state's power to discriminate against some of its citizens. In the end, the majority opinion could find no reason other than this very same primordial right. However hard they tried to pinpoint elements relative to the nature of kinship forms and to the essence of legally recognized unions, all these elements proved to be human artefacts that the law decided to adopt as prerequisites or impediments. Nonetheless, arguing that a given social practice cannot be *legally* recognized because its true essence is *legally* defined as an impediment by state law is like putting the cart before the horse. In spite of the evident clash between the level of social ontology and the one of legal construction, the majority did not formally acknowledge the foundational and finally unjustifiable role of officials who filter human social practices according to hardly neutral criteria. On the other hand, this judgment helps us understand the relevance of the blatant circularities on which it was based. The ongoing assimilation of a legal category (partnership) to a fact endowed with ontological dignity evidences that the legal language's claim is that reality should accord with legal categories. This is the chief expedient by which the law manages to (semiotically) lock up its realm in order to make the law insensitive to the facts that cannot be easily converted into the legal lexicon.

Burden and Burden v. the UK is but one instance of the juridico-political mechanism whereby state law filters social practices. Needless to say, it is easy to see that a free-floating, radical pluralism of life forms is unfeasible. The existence itself of a juridico-political system entails making decisions and (to a greater or lesser extent) distributing unequally. The existence of an orderly political community always produces iniquities and imbalances among citizens. This is the reason why this chapter should not be read as a critique of mechanisms of legal selection as such, but as an attempt to foreground a tension that traverses liberal-constitutional regimes: the tension between two rival understandings of politics that are reflected in the difference between the first and the second judgments in *Burden and Burden v. the UK*. As the first judgment in 2006 led to the same conclusions reached by the majority opinion in 2008, it is undeniable that little would have been gained in terms of a more open kinship grid. However, the first judgment, as far as I interpret it, takes issue with a potential option (the disquieting idea that siblings can form a family) and treats it as an option. The second, on the contrary, seeks to represent the relationship between siblings as a theoretical inconsistency. The first judgment gives voice to the alternative model. The second silences it. Although selective activities are inevitable, the only way to fathom and remedy their inequitable consequences is to make them plainly visible. The following chapter dwells on this tension from a different viewpoint. It does not look at how it is worked and tamed by and within institutions, but centres on an overt challenge to institutions that comes from outside them. I will discuss how religious faiths and religious normative practices are contesting the traditional accommodation of competing normativities within liberal-constitutional regimes and how the law reacts to this unsettling dynamic.

2 Juridification without institutions
Fragmenting the law

This chapter centres on two major challenges to the traditional understanding of law and the state, that is, the reviviscence of religion as a practice with normative bearings on believers' conduct and the rise of sub-state normative orderings that claim autonomy from state law. There is an obvious connection between these two phenomena. As I will argue, insofar as the *practical* side of religion comes back to the fore (against an understanding of religion as belief), it brings into question the traditional dividing line between *private* conscience and *public* behaviour. Needless to say, these are not the only societal phenomena that are posing a threat to the traditional pre-eminence of state law over other types of normativity. However, what concerns me is the link between religious practice and legal normativity. To put it differently, what distinguishes less recent forms of multiculturalism as typical features of Western liberal-constitutional states from more recent (and I believe more radical) forms of legal pluralism is that the internal normativities of cultural and religious groups seek to escape the grip of state legal orders, as group members come to believe that their internal orderings should be given more importance than the laws of official institutions. This is why I regard the connection between these two phenomena as giving rise to a noteworthy type of juridification *without* institutions. The aspect of juridification resides in the fact that cultural and religious groups contest state law in a way that puts the law at the heart of their claim to (smaller or greater) autonomy, and thus engage in a conflict against state law by means of another normativity that they believe to be a law.

Section 2.1 discusses the burgeoning hypothesis that ours is a post-secular age. However, more than the various debates on whether the label 'post-secularism' does justice to today's role of religions in public life, as I pointed out above I am interested in how religion is more and more reacquiring its salience as a practice that aims to offer guidance for conduct, and thus its norms and precepts run the risk of clashing with the norms and precepts of state law. This issue will lead me to tackle the question of legal pluralism as the idea that the law of the state is just one type of law among many others. While this major contention is supported by a good deal of theoretical and empirical analyses that I will only be able to mention in passing, in Section 2.2 my concern will be with what legal pluralism entails from the point of view of the relation between law and politics. More precisely, I will try to answer the question of whether a legal-pluralist scenario is compatible with the project of contemporary statehood, or whether the mere claim that the law of the state is but one law among many favours the fragmentation of existing political communities. While addressing this question, I will mainly look into the relations between the claim to legal autonomy and people's agency. Indeed, while this book is devoted to investigating the creative potential of people's recourse to law, my objective here is to understand what happens when people do not rely on official law and yet make claims concerning the validity and the authority of state law. This inquiry will conclude with a discussion of a type of recognition of non-state legal orderings that is able to deactivate (or at least lessen) the conflict between state and non-state laws and to make juridification an important vehicle for social and political change.

2.1 The post-secular turn

At the turn of the millennium, the public sphere of Western countries underwent a series of internal transformations that may be regarded as the concretization of what Jürgen Habermas (2006: 258) dubbed 'Böckenförde's theorem'. Habermas refers to Ernst-Wolfgang Böckenförde's merciless analysis of the shortcomings of the liberal state, or rather, the particular form of organization that emerged out of the pacification of modern confessional wars and eventually triumphed as the only imaginable political regime (Tilly 1989). By drawing on German philosopher Hermann Lübbe, Böckenförde provides an influential definition of secularization as *the withdrawal or release of an object, territory or institution from ecclesiastical and spiritual observance and control.* According to Böckenförde, the whole project of the modern state pivots on a secularist ideology, one that relegates religion to the private sphere of individual conscience and claims that the political sphere should be religiously and ethically neutral. Böckenförde's theorem advances the hypothesis that the liberal state as a religiously neutral political structure is collapsing and that the resurgence of religion is the seal of this tragic end.

I decided to start the analysis of such a deep societal and political turn with Böckenförde's critique of the secular state because it helps identify some of the key variables that are involved in this far-reaching process. Böckenförde's reading of what is known as 'secularization' has two main merits.

First, it throws light on the role that secularization played in the construction of modern states. Second, it contributes to understanding how traditional accounts of secularization postulating the existence of a link between the modern and the secular were more or less instrumental in the consolidation of state power.

To commence, Böckenförde problematizes one of the core features of the liberal conception of the secular state, that is, the idea of neutrality. Whereas the idea of 'civil religion' – or more exactly, the control over religion in order for it to serve specifically political functions – can be regarded as a *fil rouge* in Western political thinking (Beiner 2011), Böckenförde insists that states' religious neutrality was nothing other than a pretence. In fact, modern governmental centres – such as the military elites who were taking over the power of the waning political centres (the Holy Roman Empire and the Roman Church) – made a strategic use of religion in order to take spiritual matters into their own hands. As the famous principle 'cuius regio eius religio' ('whose realm, his religion') shows, the privatization of religion resulted in its *politicization*: it was the *private* choice of the ruler that decided what the official, *public* religion of state would be. Böckenförde's portrayal presents the new governmental centres as an attempt to put religious matters under their sway in order to foster a brand-new understanding of the relation between politics and law, which was at odds with pre-modern ideas. By severing the ties with any metaphysical premises, the law could be represented as the worldly product of a sovereign will. Conversely, lawgivers could claim this law to be religiously neutral precisely because its only source was their sovereign will.

In short, the rise of modern states was hallmarked by a (somewhat deliberately) ambiguous attitude towards religion. On the one hand, faith was downgraded to a non-political affair pertaining to citizens as private individuals. On the other hand, the state as a political form was essentially based on the ruler's official recognition of one religion. Nonetheless, according to Böckenförde, the project of a neutral state was doomed to fail. Nationalism as a substitute for the previous religious and ethical bonds turned out to be unsuccessful in the long run. As a result, the liberal state proved unable to keep its promises. As the striking renaissance of religion in contemporary politics testifies, secularism was nourished by presuppositions that it could not itself guarantee, and states at present are looking for renewed metaphysical supports. This is the gist of the Böckenförde theorem.

Before I examine this hypothesis and explore the paths of so-called 'post-secularism', which according to a good deal of scholars captures the existing conditions of most Western states, it may be of help to take a quick look at what preceded the post-secular and to clarify some key terms, such as *secular*, *secularization* and *secularism*.

According to a widespread, well-established view, secularization and modernity are essentially linked: the latter triggered the former while the former became the heart of the latter. This view was started by noble fathers of sociology Émile Durkheim and Max Weber. Although their methods and conclusions are scarcely reconcilable, they agreed that the signature of the modern era is a comprehensive revision of its relationship to religion. Durkheim sees the marginalization of religion as the transition from traditional to modern societies. While the traditional societies hinged on forms of solidarity and community bonds rooted in strong collective feelings based on religion, modern societies dispensed with any type of solidarity that entailed transcendent or divine elements. If modern societies did not discard the sacred, the sacred remarkably changed its face. On his part, Weber spoke of disenchantment as an image of the world that does not make room for magical elements and is driven by a process of rationalization. In sum, despite substantial differences on the role and essence of religion, both these giants of modern social theory concur on the innate connection between modernity and secularization.

However, in the last few decades a series of innovative analyses and new meta-histories have been advanced that seek to provide alternative narratives of events and developments related to secularization and to offer a novel view of the role of religion in the contemporary world.

Charles Taylor (2009) nicely captures the links among secularization, the privatization of religious experience and the creation of the state as the dominant political form. The state sanctified the 'self-sufficiency of the secular', which was inherently based on the ban on religion's public role. Faith had to be confined to the private sphere whereas the state had to be rooted in a coherent, self-sufficient social morality with no transcendent reference. Interestingly, Taylor notes that this movement brought about a stronger demand for shared political identity and minimized the pluralism that former political forms had been able to accommodate. If other types of regimes, from ancient empires to medieval princedoms, were comprised of different populations with different religious allegiances and legal customs, the modern state claimed to provide a clear-cut and conclusive answer to the question of what and for whom the state is for. There needed to be a common and agreed upon basis of identification, that is, the people, with a strong collective identity, which in turn required a firm commitment of single individuals to one another in a joint political project. To account for this mutation, Taylor (2007) advances the notion of 'immanent frame', namely a bounded order, devoid of transcendence, where the experience of the individual can do without reference to something that 'goes beyond': a radical change of our social imagery (Taylor 2010).

These insights shed some first light on the meaning of 'secular'. It would be a mistake to think of it as the upshot of rationalization and modernization vis-à-vis religious obscurantism. As Taylor argues, the immanent frame was the creation of specific religious actors, or rather, the consequence of providential deism and exclusive humanism fostered *within* orthodox Christianity. If this is the case, then the secular did not emerge out of either the disappearance or the privatization of religion as such. 'Secular' first and foremost denotes an internal political transformation of European Christianity (Asad 2003; Casanova 2006), whereby religion itself, or better, particular forms of the Christian faith, gave way to other types of identification and public morality. In effect, Talal Asad (2003: 192) reminds us that the concept of 'the secular' was elaborated within a theological discourse, as the term 'secularization' 'at first denoted a legal transition from monastic life (*regularis*) to the life of canons (*saecularis*)'. José Casanova (2006: 10) reinforces this conclusion by arguing that 'the formation of the secular is itself inextricably linked with the internal transformation of European Christianity'. Even within Europe, it would be better to speak of differentiated, heterogeneous patterns of secularization, as the difference between the models of 'secularism' and 'laïcité' illustrates (Roy 2007).

This understanding of the secular leads to a more refined view of secularization as something that never really occurred in the forms and modes described by the supporters of the traditional view. To put it another way, clear borders should be drawn between *secularization as a phenomenon* and *secularization as a narrative*. Roughly speaking, the former is a complex and variegated set of struggles among institutional actors over the legitimacy of political and legal claims; the latter is the way in which the discourse about the modern state has long been framed – to wit, the progressive exit of religion from the political sphere as a means to draw modern confessional wars to a close and the transformation of faith into a private, individual matter of conscience.

If this alternative account holds, it would be a serious mistake to account for secularization as a phenomenon in the light of secularization as a narrative. This is a fallacy that Casanova (2009) calls 'secularism'. He advances the distinction between *secularism as a statecraft principle*, which has to do with secularization as a phenomenon, and *secularism as an ideology*, or rather, a theory of what 'religion' is or does. In the first sense, secularism is a multiple set of strategies deployed by states to bring about a separation between the sphere of religion and the sphere of political action. In the second sense, secularism bears an ideological connotation, in that it played a crucial part in the spread of the secularization narrative. Secularism as an ideology served as a teleology of religious decline that operated as a self-fulfilling prophecy (van der Veer 2009). In this respect, it was laden with utopian and quasi-religious elements that fed statehood and subsequent nationalist ideologies.

In substance, contrary to the standard view at which I hinted above, this interpretation considers the transient relation between secularization and modernity as instrumental in the establishment of the state and the justification of its authority. Therefore, the assumption that the history of modernity coincides with the history of the state turns out to be flawed. The state did not come about as the enlightened exit from the subjection to religious institutions, the progressive creation of a public, neutral, lay political sphere, and the setting and maintaining of stable borders between this and the private sphere where religion should be confined.

Without a doubt, this more recent perspective has rapidly made inroads into current political and social theory. Some of those who used to believe in the link between the rise of modernity and the decline in religiosity have revised their initial thoughts. This turn of mind is epitomized by Peter Berger's (1998) admission that the big mistake, which he shared with those who worked in this area in the second part of the 20th century, was to believe that modernity is synonymous with the demise of religion. This is why a good deal of scholars (e.g. Caputo 2001; De Vries and Sullivan 2006; Habermas 2010) dwelling on the place of religion in today's political arena have adopted the telling label 'post-secular' to denote the condition of existing societies, where the political weight of religion is undeniable. Nonetheless, the meanings and nuances of this label are several (Beckford 2012), as it all depends on the positions that those who invoke it take on the standard narrative of secularization. Let me examine a few alternatives.

According to those who for the most part still hold on to a liberal theoretical framework, the main problem we need to tackle at present is how to rework the filter between the private and the public realms. Habermas is the champion of this perspective. As the story goes, the confinement of religion to a merely private domain turned out to be unsustainable both for believers and non-believers. Within the framework of liberal states, members of religious communities have long been forced to live a double life – private and public – and to adopt a public language with which they did not always feel at ease in order to conform to the requirements of secular law. On their part, non-religious citizens today prove unable to carry the burden of a post-metaphysical condition, where the rationalization of the world has given way to new forms of political rationality – such as, for example, neoliberalism – which are eroding all resources of social solidarity and favouring the upsurge of individualism. Habermas (2010) warns us that an entirely new relationship between the secular and the religious spheres is about to reshape both our conception and practice of politics.

Habermas explains that what the state was able to overcome – the disastrous consequences of confessional wars – is likely to make a comeback: such wars are being repeated not only in the relation between the

Western and the Islamic worlds, but also in that between citizens affiliated with religious groups and citizens who have no religious allegiances. In Habermas' view, this scenario should urge liberal democratic states to even up the unfair asymmetry in the obligations they impose on religious and non-religious citizens, especially when it comes to justifying claims within the public sphere. He thinks that a mutual learning process is likely to stem from this predicament. On the one hand, religious citizens and organizations are required to grant full recognition to the public sphere as a venue where no religious truth can be foisted upon anyone. On the other hand, secular institutions should cease forcing citizens who belong to religious groups to reframe their claims in a non-religious lexicon and should recognize that religious claims can make a significant contribution to clarifying controversial questions of principle.

This first formulation of post-secularism, however, owes much to the crystallized view of secularization I brought into question in the previous pages. The central tenet is that, as the ability of liberal states to cope with pluralism is waning, religion is becoming cause for concern and conflict. On this account, the pressing question is how to deal with religiously inspired opinions when it comes to debating shared issues of public policy. According to some critics (see, for example, Bader 2012; Beckford 2012), this approach hinders adequate understanding of the role of religion in today's political communities. For everything is read through the lens of the traditional liberal view that pits the state against religious groups.

This type of post-secularism is vitiated from the very beginning, as it does not go much farther than John Rawls', the champion of political liberalism. Rawls (2005) contends that religious beliefs can well be accommodated in the political arena insofar as they are reasonable in *liberal* terms. In the many debates on the issue over which secular and religious provisions collide (from ritual slaughter to school dress codes), the bearers of what he labels 'comprehensive doctrines', whether religious or not, can hardly avoid introducing arguments based on controversial views. Yet, they are required to do so in compliance with what Rawls calls 'the *proviso*', postulating that reasonable religious or non-religious views can be introduced in public political discussion provided that in due course proper political reasons – and not reasons given solely by these views – are presented that are sufficient to support whatever the views introduced are said to support (on the place Rawls assigns religion, see Bailey and Gentile 2014). Despite a few differences in Habermas' and Rawls' analyses (see Ferrara 2009), they agree that the solution to potential clashes between religious and non-religious views in Western liberal societies is to be found within the frame of the public sphere, where conflicts can be turned into exchanges of reasons.

Generally speaking, a major flaw that affects these theoretical paradigms, as well as others inspired by them, is the persistent reduction of religion to a matter of belief and the neglect of its practical, behavioural, interactional side (Stychin 2009). Religion is not (or at least not only) a set of beliefs, it is a *practice*. Or better, religion is embedded in a practice that is the cradle of a more complex set of beliefs and conducts. Its accommodation requires a deeper rethinking of the legal and political practices of liberal states. This is why I believe it is worth exploring alternative understandings of post-secularism, which place emphasis on different traits of religious practices and foresee different societal developments.

A sound account of post-secularism that does not suffer either from an ambiguous connection with the secularization narrative or from a narrow conception of religion as the ultimate authority on every human and non-human aspect is Ingolf Dalferth's (2010) analysis of the place of religion after the collapse of the myth of secular modernity. The first point Dalferth makes is that it is one thing to say that a state has to be neutral, quite another to say that a society has to be neutral. The former is a principle inspiring specific types of non-discriminatory policies, the latter is just a misleading view of society. No modern civil society has ever been neutral. With reference to Asad (2003) and Taylor (2007), Dalferth argues that no simple or unambiguous development from pre-secular through secular to post-secular societies can be traced. No complete expulsion of religion from the public life of society or the individual life of its citizens has ever been achieved. Hence, the first step to a comprehensive understanding of post-secularism requires rejecting traditional views that claim to single out clear-cut stages or evolutions.

According to Dalferth, the appropriate background against which a comprehensive understanding of post-secularism can be developed is the theory of social differentiation. By capitalizing on Niklas Luhmann's system theory, he describes society as a plurality of publics (politics, economy, science, religion, law, art, the media, etc.), each of which is constituted by characteristic modes of interaction and communication. On this account, there is an important distinction to be made: the political sphere is only a sphere of the broader society, that is, the totality of socially differentiated spheres. If this is the case, Dalferth contends, genuinely post-secular states are those that, unlike secular states, cease defining themselves as neutral or non-neutral vis-à-vis religion. They simply do not take a stance as to the religious allegiances of their citizens. This is a remarkable shift. Indeed, Dalferth goes on by saying whether religious or non-religious views can be justified with recourse to public reasons is for individuals to determine, not the state. Hence, a truly post-secular state is indifferent to questions of religion or non-religion, and not just neutral. Whether there are many religious or non-religious associations in society, the state does refrain from defining its relations to them in any particular way. In sum, a genuinely post-secular state is one in which a proper secularization process can eventually take place – that is, one whereby the state refuses to understand and think of itself in relation to any religion so that religion may actually and freely occupy its proper place within society.

More nuanced and sociologically sounder analyses of this sort have led scholars to reject uncomplicated allegiances to a secular platform that simply rule post-secularism out as a form of disguised conservatism. There is no such thing as a clear dividing line between the secular and the post-secular. A stark example is Saba Mahmood's (2005) ethnography of the women's mosque movement in Cairo, which aims to debunk the ideological foundations of Western secular feminism. Mahmood questions poststructuralist feminist approaches insofar as they conceptualize agency merely in terms of subversion and resignification of available social norms. However, she contends the binary subordination/subversion in some contexts does not hold. The way to effect social change is both historically and culturally specific. Accordingly, it can well be the case that what from a certain vantage point appears as passivity and docility, from another vantage point proves to be a specific form of agency – one that cannot be understood without reference to specific discourses and structures of subordination.

Mahmood's study provides further evidence that at present theories that engage with issues such as gender and sexual oppression, traditionally anchored to secular visions of politics, can no longer stick to a secularist theoretical grid (see Conclusion). At least, they can no longer take 'secular' in a self-evident sense (Braidotti 2008). As Mahmood insists, the renewed link between political action and religious spirituality feeds non-secularist visions of political activity that make room for new creative alternatives, based on a more comprehensive notion of *religious agency*. The careful reconsideration of the relationship between agency and its context calls for a revision of the deep-seated secular assumptions that have long dominated critical and feminist theories (Bracke 2008). Religious agency should not be regarded as 'defective', unless scholars want to re-confine gender and sexual minorities engaging in religious practices to a condition of social 'illegibility' whereby they are deemed to be under the yoke of an oblivious subjugation. Religious agency and religious subjectivities need to be rethought and re-read against new theoretical constellations that allow capturing the forces that shape and drive social agents. They can claim active ownership over the religious practices that shape their identity.

This notion of an agency that takes place in contexts of potential or actual oppression, such as conservative, heterosexist or gender-biased religious organizations, does away with the opposition of structures and practices.

Active, conscious agency is the entry point for practices to change structures so as to make room for 'religio-spiritual approaches' (Aune 2015) that are context-specific, bound up with the religion as a practice, and naturally interactive. There are two main advantages to this view. First, religions, and religious organizations in particular, can no longer be considered as static structures insensitive to social change. Rather, they are shifting collections of people who engage in complex sets of actions and discourses that contribute to the definition of the collective as a whole (Ammerman 1997). Second, agents are acknowledged to be active factors of internal change as they produce alternative, competing accounts of the contexts in which they are situated. The case of Catholic women investigated by Laura Leming (2007) illustrates how women constantly negotiate their 'place' and 'space' in Catholicism by way of strategies that are meant to create social networks that recognize and encourage the strength and relevance of women. Or the case of Israeli Modern-Orthodox Agunah activists who engage in highly politicized collective feminist resistance as *religious* actors working for *religious* ends (Zion-Waldoks 2015). Or the case of queer subjectivities in mainstream Christian denominations who perceive their battle for integration as a '*raison d'être*' as well as an attempt to forge a queer Christian identity that turns 'the discourse of shame and silence . . . into a narrative of pride and expression' (O'Brien 2004: 194). These phenomena mobilize a transformative force 'from within' that gives life to context-specific ways of navigating clashes and contradictions. This challenges conventional dichotomies like sexuality/religion, resistance/submission and autonomy/dependence.

Based on the analysis above, a more appropriate notion of post-secularism can be advanced, one that gets rid of the identification of modernity and secularism and proves more sensitive to the actual, distinct contexts where religious practices take place. In such a new meta-history of post-secularism, the history of religion is severed from the history of the state, while both are contextualized as variable factors in the rich tapestry of human action: dissimilar types of social differentiation lead to dissimilar relationships between society and politics, politics and religion, religion and society. While staunchly secularist visions risk being the carrier of strongly normative, and at times oppressive, visions of the political role religion ought to play, in some social contexts religious practices can actually serve as a vehicle for far-reaching change. At the same time, however, this new meta-history subtracts religion (at least from an analytical perspective) from manipulative strategies that, not unlike the secularist ideology, make a political use of religion. For they detach the element of practice/culture/identity from that of faith and in doing so give life to new forms of integralism (Roy 2007).

In conclusion, the new relationship among religion, the political sphere and the social domain, informed by a nuanced understanding of the role of religious practices in today's world, should rather be conducive to a revision of how Western constitutional regimes accommodate religion beyond the fragile principle of liberal neutrality. With the re-emergence of *religions as practices*, which the distinction between the private and the public sphere obliterated, the sharp separation of state and society seems no longer sustainable. This is why I believe the discussion of post-secularism calls for a farther-reaching discussion of how the legal systems of contemporary liberal states interact with other forms of normativity. This is the issue that I tackle in the subsequent section.

2.2 Fragmented jurisdictions and legal pluralities

Numerous studies in a variety of academic fields insist that contemporary political communities are characterized by a *de facto* condition of legal pluralism (two influential examples in the voluminous literature are Berman 2007 and Tamanaha 2008 – yet I would like to note that my focus in this section will be 'classic legal pluralism' and not 'global legal pluralism'; for a critical juxtaposition between these two paradigms see Croce and Goldoni 2015). One might be tempted to conclude that John Griffiths' (1986) pioneering diagnosis was right. Not only does legal pluralism prove a widespread state of affairs, as individuals in the same geo-historical context abide by more than one system of rules; more than that, it is the best descriptive conception of law. In sum, both conceptually and pragmatically, legal pluralism appears to be a fact. But what does it mean? What is it that the connection between the qualifier 'legal' and the noun 'pluralism' signifies? Is it the case that the legal monism of modern and late modern Western jurisprudence simply played out as a collective illusion and its state-centric ideology as an effective weapon for political elites to get hold of every sphere of society? While some leading scholars, more or less openly and more or less sympathetically, hint at this conclusion (Galanter 1981; Grossi 2010), I believe the picture is more nuanced.

To penetrate this picture, a first indispensable step is to spell out the meaning of what is becoming a buzzword (see also Melissaris and Croce 2017). As far as I can see, there are two main routes to address the issue of legal pluralism. They tease out an inborn tension that affects its conceptualization. These two routes can be summarized into one question: is legal pluralism a theoretical device or is it a concrete state of things? As I will argue, while these aspects cannot be disentangled from one another in any easy manner, it is important to distinguish them at least conceptually.

The history of legal pluralism as a conceptual stance can be traced back to a small number of eminent scholars of the early 20th century, among whom were German legal sociologist Eugen Ehrlich, Polish anthropologist Bronisław Malinowski, Italian jurist Santi Romano and Dutch jurist Cornelis van Vollenhoven. The puzzle they were seeking to unravel was the inadequacy of the concept of law produced in a scholarly environment dominated by state-centred, monist legal theories. This problem can be split in two major claims – a conceptual and a heuristic one – typical of state-based theories. The first, conceptual, claim was that the general phenomenon of law could be reduced to the law of the state, that is, the legal systems that had been produced by modern governmental agencies between the 18th and the 19th centuries. In this sense, theories of *state* law were commonly taken to be *general* theories of law. The second, heuristic, claim was that these conceptualizations of law were claimed to be able to reveal important elements of the basic structure of all societies. In particular, they could help scholars determine whether or not a given society was based on a legal (or law-like) structure. In one way or another, former pluralist theorists came to the conclusion that the conceptual and the heuristic claims of state-based theories had to be scaled down. They believed that stretching the Western concept of law for it to cover either past legal traditions or non-Western legal realities was tantamount to distorting alternative normative entities and projecting onto them a vision of law that did not reflect their experience. The law of past or non-Western populations can only be cognized with the aid of concepts produced within those very traditions.

At face value, pluralists' reaction to state-centred legal theories might seem to be akin to contextualist views in the never-ending dispute over the limitedness of one's conceptual grid vis-à-vis the other's frame of significance and form of life. To mention a well-known example in the epistemology of social sciences, in his defence of the rationality of the Azande's understanding of witchcraft, Peter Winch (1964) pointed out that, in any system of judgement, any single judgement depends on the ensemble of beliefs and practices on which it is premised. In this light, the idea of straightforwardly comparing alternative forms of life and, even worse, putting them in a hierarchy, is a symptom of blindness to the 'point' of a population's 'system of conventions' (Winch 1964: 322). In Winch's view, alien systems of conventions cannot be accessed through one's original set of beliefs and practices. For it involves a learning process that grants access to 'different possibilities of making sense of human life, different ideas about the possible importance that the carrying out of certain activities may take on for a man' (Winch 1964: 321). If applied to legal theorizing, no conception of law can be stretched to cover all instances of legal normativity. Much more heed should be paid to the indigenous, native conceptions that animate a given legal experience.

Still, I think such a general invitation to relativize Western claims to universality cannot be deemed to be the hallmark of legal pluralism. Although greater sensitivity to non-Western socio-cultural experiences and the need to produce flexible instruments of inquiry are typical traits of legal-pluralist scholarship, legal pluralism should not be reduced to a more cautious reflection on the structural limits of one's native conceptions and the risks of objectifying unfamiliar legal experiences. Much deeper than that, the major argument some legal pluralists offer is that the conception of Western law that Western theorists have developed is gravely mistaken – not only as a heuristic tool, but also as a general conceptualization of the legal phenomenon in the West. In fact, this conception is entirely based on one aspect of the legal practice and almost exclusively centred on one geo-historical configuration of legal normativity. As I hinted in the previous section, from 18th-century Enlightenment onwards, new elites of legislators and jurists struggled to get rid of the remnants of medieval and pre-modern legal conceptions and practices to foster a novel view where the law-maker was granted a pivotal role (Grossi 2010: Chapter 2). This novel, top-down view was founded on a pyramidal understanding of legal sovereignty, on a new hierarchy among law-making and law-applying agencies, and on a new conception of the sources of law. The law came to be understood as a technique to use force based on state agencies' monopoly on coercion. This view infiltrated all interstices of legal theorizing to the extent that most Western scholars believed there was no law unless dedicated agencies were put in place that could produce and enforce legal rules. Against this view, pluralists like Ehrlich (2009) and Romano (2017) claimed that even in Western settings the legal phenomenon is far broader than the special technique developed by state agencies to secure peace. It embraces embryonic forms of normativity regulating everyday individuals' conducts and group dynamics. The law of the state is a type of law among a variety of other laws.

However, even this more fine-grained understanding of legal pluralism fails to clear up an ambiguity that besets its conceptualization. As I noted at the outset, it is by no means clear whether the claims legal pluralists raise are of a descriptive or a normative type. The first type of claim about the need to narrow down the heuristic value of Western theories falls under the scope of a descriptive paradigm that seems compatible with more common views of state law. For it could in principle be accommodated in state-based paradigms that acknowledge the epistemological pitfalls of Western theoretical frames. In this reading, a fruitful conjunction of classical and legal-pluralist theories is likely to further the aim of producing a nuanced and historically more alert description of the various geo-historical situations under scrutiny. Instead, the second type of claim purports to give the lie to all of the theories that see state law as a uniform, monolithic entity, and accordingly depicts state-centrism as a political ideology. This latter claim becomes *normative*, in that it makes the case for those forms of non-state laws that have long (and, in this frame, unjustly) been dispossessed of their value of 'legality' to the advantage of state law. It can be viewed as a radical politicization of theory as the idea itself that state law is a common body of rules that overrides other non-legal rules is belied.

In the current juridico-political context of Western polities, this ambiguity is intertwined with the transition I discussed in the previous section. As religion is being taken out of the ivory tower of one's private conscience, its aspect of normative practice is thrust into the limelight. Religion is no longer a mere set of beliefs, but purports to provide guidance on how one should conduct oneself in one's daily activities. This element is thoroughly discussed in Ayelet Shachar's (2001) work on multicultural jurisdictions, one of the most influential revisions of multiculturalism. She advances the notion of '*nomoi* communities' to refer to religiously defined groups that regard religion as providing rules for conduct relevant to everyday life in one's political community. Shachar's notion captures those minority groups, organized primarily along ethnic, racial, tribal or national-origin lines, whose 'members share a comprehensive and distinguishable worldview that extends to creating a law for the community' (Shachar 2001: 2).

For my purposes in this book, what is particularly relevant is the legal import of religious practices. As religion exits the realm of one's private life, it lays claims to the regulation of believers' public life and undercuts such traditional binaries as private/public and cultural/political. The *legal* factor that characterized religion before the rise of the state (see Section 2.1) has now become decisive to the extent that it challenges the uniqueness of state law as a common regulatory frame for all citizens of liberal states. One could go so far as to say that this junction of the religious and the legal distinguishes genuine circumstances of legal pluralism from more traditional accommodations of cultural and religious difference. As Carol Greenhouse (1998: 66) notes, the specifically *legal* nuance that pluralism takes on in contemporary liberal societies calls for 'an alternative approach' that foregrounds 'the processes by which law comes to be a sign of cultural identity, as well as the aspects of cultural solidarity that are *not* recognized in the sign systems the law commands'. Based on the renewed link between the rules providing guidance for conduct and the complex tapestry of religious identity, legal pluralism ceases to be a theory of law and turns into a much broader (political) view of social order and the relationship between the legal sphere and the other spheres of social life.

Some theorists of multiculturalism grasp this crucial twist and warn against the perils of a truly legal-pluralist scenario. In an article that aims to dispel a few misconstructions about multicultural policies, Jan Pakulski (2014: 28) avers that there are radicalized versions of multiculturalism promoting not only cultural pluralism but also elements relative to political organization and even 'elements of legal code'. He continues to say that accepting this form of diversity goes well beyond the realm of culture, lifestyles and identities, and could thus 'be blamed for ethno-religious fragmentation, particularism and even separatism' (Pakulski 2014: 28). That the crux of the matter is how the legal factor alters the practical relevance of culture and religion is made even clearer by Bryan S. Turner and Berna Zengin Arslan's (2011) text on the interplay between Shari'a and Western law in Western states. They argue that without a doubt there was a time in Europe in which pluralism was a state of things whereby different normative orderings enjoyed various degrees of autonomy and could be enforced by a variety of legal or quasi-legal bodies. However, the modern state, they continue to say, has irretrievably changed the legal landscape in a Weberian sense. Still today, the law is a normative ordering enforced by state agencies that claim sovereignty over a given territory. In the light of that, Turner and Arslan argue that legal pluralism can well be regarded as a condition in which different 'bodies of law' compete with each other; and yet they maintain that we cannot afford to give up the idea of the state having the ultimate sanction over legal jurisdiction, even in the presence of a variety of sub-state legal bodies.

But what is really the element of political disruption that legal pluralism is accused of bringing about? The disruptive element was pithily described by Carl Schmitt ([1930]2000), as early as 1930, in the essay 'State Ethics and the Pluralist State'. Here he muses on the reason why a truly pluralist state of things cannot be imprisoned in the comforting area of individuals' private conscience and publicly tamed by the secularist binary private/public. In effect, as the practical relevance of religion in today's liberal states, pluralism is hardly something pertaining to the non-political sphere. As Schmitt puts it, this type of pluralism is of the highest political relevance because it favours the construction of political allegiances that pose a threat to the allegiance to the state. It goes without saying that Schmitt's view on this matter owes a debt to his understanding of the political as the sphere where a community reaches the utmost degree of intensity. The political is that in the light of which friends gather around a substantive homogeneity that permits them to distinguish themselves from the enemies (for a comprehensive discussion of Schmitt's view of the political and its changes over time see Croce and Salvatore 2013). However, he makes a case that goes beyond the borders of his own theorization.

Schmitt ([1930]2000) laments that the advocates of pluralism – more specifically, he has in mind British champions of the pluralist state G.D.H. Cole and Harold I. Laski (see Runciman 1997: 162–194) – make the mistake of putting social groups and the state on an equal footing. It is as if the public arena of the state were nothing but one of the dimensions of life that citizens live in differentiated societies along with other dimensions that have to do with the various aspects of their lives: the school, the workplace, the church, and so on. The political sphere being only one element of citizens' multifaceted biography in complex societies, the state 'becomes a social group or association existing at best side-by-side with, but on no account above, the other associations' (Schmitt [1930]2000: 301). Schmitt's reflection is relevant to my purposes here because he does not intend to deny the multiplicity of spheres that comprise a society. He does recognize that all societies are to some extent communities of sub-communities. However, he points out that a certain type of pluralism can be truly detrimental to the very existence of an overarching political community to which all citizens must be equally tied. In this regard, what he holds responsible for the spread of such a harmful pluralism is the idea that the state is a neutral, mediatory power that oversees the balance of groups and prevents clashes among them. In brief, his criticism boils down to the argument that, however strong one's connection to a group might be, not all groups decide on what counts as 'normal' in one's whole life. In a less Schmittian jargon, I can say that, despite the multiple identities that individuals can take on in the course of their life, the group that definitely affects their self-understanding and self-perception turns out to be their *political* group: it moulds the grid of intelligibility through which individuals experience the world, value things and assess conducts (see Croce and Salvatore 2017).

While mulling over this dilemma, such recognized experts in contemporary pluralism as Ran Hirschl and Shachar (2009) appear to agree with Schmitt that what is at stake today is precisely the state's claim to serve as a common framework, an ultimate horizon. This radical challenge, they argue, makes the conventional jargon of tolerance and societal pluralism evaporate. Liberal institutions and liberal citizens are confronted with a situation that reflects

> a more foundational power struggle between competing systems of knowledge and interpretation: the earthly, human-enacted constitution and the claim to speak in a vernacular of a revealed or divine authority. When faced with this kind of challenge, even the most generous and even-handed officials of the state are structurally not in a position to rule from a 'point of view from nowhere'.
>
> (Hirschl and Shachar 2009: 2537)

If this analysis holds true, it seems reasonable to conclude that *legal* pluralism, much more than traditional multiculturalism, is a societal phenomenon that threatens the political nature of the overarching association called 'state'. As Schmitt has it, when religion and culture claim to regulate the practical life of a group, the latter *ipso facto* turns into a political entity (I expand on this point in Croce 2017a). Nonetheless, it is my contention that, when the political nature of legal pluralism comes to the surface, this major challenge can be faced in such a way that state law and legal pluralism may coexist.

As discussed in various strands of literature, this can be achieved in two primary ways. To explore them, it is worth looking into a heated debate on what form contemporary legal pluralism could/should take in liberal political communities. This debate revolves around the key question of how a pluralism that defies one of the main principles of liberalism – that is, the traditional separation between the private and the public – can be reconciled with the projects of liberal politics and democratic constitutionalism. A good entry point is Gordon Woodman's (2006, 2008) discussion of what type of relationship could/should exist between the state and groups that claim to exert jurisdictional authority over their members and even hold the view that their rules are more authoritative than the state's (at least in some key spheres of the group's life). Woodman outlines different options for the state to develop a relationship with the laws that are followed and accepted within a given sub-state. In particular, he singles out two types of recognition processes, which are each meant to encourage or give effect to another non-state law: *institutional* and *normative* recognition.

When a state adopts the first type of recognition, it acknowledges the existence of institutions and structures that belong to non-state laws and recognizes the legal validity and legal effects of the activities they carry out. Such an institutional recognition restricts the jurisdiction of state agencies and allows non-state ones to wield authority over those areas from which the state withdraws. Even though in this case, Woodman explains, the relative competences of state and non-state agencies are formally established, institutional recognition can in some circumstances operate tacitly, when the institutions of state law decline to exercise functions in cases in which those of another law are acting. On the contrary, normative recognition does not presuppose any restriction on the state jurisdiction. Rather, the state recognizes some of the norms of the non-state law and takes it upon itself to apply them. From a formal viewpoint, I could say that the norms of the recognized law are replicated within state law. Generally speaking, state law can accept some of the norms of another law in a given area but can establish some sort of principle that excludes the recognition of other norms which are believed to be at odds with relevant parts of state law.

Woodman distinguishes two scenarios that follow from either one or the other type of recognition. Institutional recognition is likely to lead to a condition of what he calls 'deep legal pluralism', that is to say, a distinct set of laws with their own different sources of authority and separate jurisdictions.

Normative recognition is likely to eventuate in a 'state law pluralism', in which a (by and large) uniform state law would make room for distinct bodies of norms that have their origin in different normative contexts. Shachar (2008) critically accounts for deep legal pluralism in terms of 'privatized diversity'. She claims that the demise of the rigid binary private/public is being followed by a polarization that sees the defenders of a one-law-for-all model as opposed to a 'private justice' model. In another text (Shachar 2012), she qualifies this model as 'the *culture override* approach', in the sense that culture should be recognized as a factor or personal element that trumps other allegiances or forms of belonging, even when disputes are to be adjudicated in public courts. The advocates of this approach oppose those who think the obverse, or rather, that culture or religion should play no part whatsoever in the administration of justice. The main claim that the defenders of the culture override approach advance is that the traditional strategies of liberal institutions, based on state neutrality and the depoliticization of difference, place an undue burden on those who believe cultural or religious matters do not fit easily into the cramped space of the private. Accordingly, they demand that public, state-sponsored efforts to accommodate diversity should be dismissed because liberal inclusion revealed itself as a *genuinely political* strategy to silence the needs and interests of cultural and religious groups. Consequently, rather than inclusion, members of these groups should pursue *exclusion from* liberal institutions, while the state should permit them to be subjected to different legal regimes according to their 'personal status'.

At this point, it is worth clarifying what 'personal status' means in this context. A legal system where rules attach to people according to some distinctive traits (such as race, colour, sex, faith and/or profession) is called 'personal law system'. As Jeffrey Redding (2007) explains, personal law systems date back to Roman law, where legal rules did not unfold along territorial lines, but varied according to specific elements of one's individual biography. Personal law systems are still in place in many non-Western areas. For example, India's legal system, though secular and based on a written constitution, distinguishes citizens according to communal religious identities – faiths as diverse as Hinduism, Islam, Christianity and Sikhism (see, for example, Menski 2010b; Menski 2011). In other words, throughout the history of Western political communities as well as in present non-Western social realities, there have been many examples of legal systems in which the law attaches to persons – a law that people bring with them when they move from one location or territory to another. When states recognize the validity and bindingness of these laws, their systems are instances of deep legal pluralism, in that different legal rules are binding upon different people within the same geographical unit, so much so that people are *de facto* sorted 'into various legal regimes depending on the "type of person" involved' (Redding 2007: 957).

Shachar offers the persuasive argument that the straightforward opposition between the idea of one law for all, wilfully blind to cultural and religious factors, and the model of a personal law system, where groups are governed by laws of their own, does nothing but replicate at a higher level the conventional 'either/or' model of secularist statehood. *Either* minority groups yield to state law, which guarantees liberal rights and freedoms, *or* they withdraw from this neutral platform to subject themselves to private orderings that might comprise illiberal or gender-biased values. This opposition is doubly hazardous. On the part of the state, it could be a way to evade responsibility to protect more vulnerable citizens. On the part of minority groups, it prompts authorities within them to charge members who are not willing to waive state protection with being disloyal and disrespectful to their group. Moreover, as Samia Bano (2008) remarks, not only does the either/or opposition favour a polarization that relieves the state of its responsibilities and creates internal enemies within the group; no less importantly, this opposition betrays the original spirit of legal pluralism and its critique of Westerners' heuristic hubris. In fact, the very same image of fixed and homogenous groups that confront the state and demand the right to be governed by a separate body of law entails the idea of entities that are recognizable on account of their mechanisms of control and enforcement. Bano warns that this image obscures the many narratives and discourses – other than the objectified and reified ones favoured by the opposition state/ groups – which make a group what it is. To put it more bluntly, the state/ group binary portrayal of two internally consistent and uniform entities neglects the legal-pluralist conclusion that every social phenomenon is a 'plurality of pluralities' (Menski 2010a: 6). But how can a form of legal pluralism be preserved in such a way that this pitfall is avoided?

It is one thing to say that deep legal pluralism can be harmful to vulnerable subjects, quite another to revert to a liberal model oblivious to legal pluralism. As Bano comments, the view of the people involved, also of potentially disadvantaged individuals, is far from consistent. She sets out to examine a specific case study, that is, the voice of Muslim women with regard to the issue of Shari'a councils and their jurisdictional autonomy. Bano maintains that women are sensitive to the opinion of those who believe that secular state law fails to adequately address matrimonial disputes for Muslims living in Britain. For example, under Muslim law women are permitted a divorce without the consent of their husbands. In this case, a religious scholar is called upon to determine which kind of divorce can be issued. However, Bano claims that at this point we are faced with two crucial variables that are usually underplayed in the either/or portrayal.

First, the legal body that is supposed to take over is hardly homogenous and coherent. It is by no means easy to navigate the enormous diversity of the Islamic normative repertoire. Bano (2008: 298) writes that Shari'a councils do not embody 'a singular set of shared cultural and religious norms', but are 'imbued with different interpretations of Islamic legal principles and differing power relations, revealing internal contestation, conflict and change among and between them'.

Second, even less homogenous and coherent is the point of view of women who show both hopes and concerns with regard to Shari'a councils. Bano's empirical study as well as the literature she draws on bring out the productive and workable fuzziness of sub-state normative life. There is little doubt that most often these informal adjudicative arenas are male dominated, hold conservative views on the role of women in society, and are concerned with reconciling the parties (the focus being on matrimonial disputes). However, it appears that some women do find them useful – although some of those interviewed by Bano experienced discomfort and unease, as they were regarded by religious scholars as potentially dangerous participants on account of their unwillingness to be reconciled. Much in the same vein as those who emphasize the context-specific effectiveness of women's and queer subjectivities' agency in religious associations (see Section 2.1), Bano (2008: 301) underlines that through informal processes of dispute resolution some women are 'able to challenge cultural practices such as forced marriage as "un-Islamic" and antithetical to the values of "being a Muslim"'.

In short, the liberal dividing wall between the public and the private just as well as the opposite view of a privatized justice foster an opposition state/group that conceals elements of promising contradiction. For example, the internal heterogeneity of groups, the variety of discourses and narratives that feed their tradition, the existence of imbalances of power among group members, the narrative of minorities within minorities, the fissures opened by the committed involvement of disadvantaged subjects. On the one hand, the administration of justice cannot be entirely devolved to sub-state group authorities, because this would contribute to the reinforcement of existing hierarchies and the subjection of internal minorities. On the other hand, the bare neglect of non-state normative orderings and their alternative dispute settling procedures would be utterly insensitive to the demands of people whose life is deeply embedded in cultural and religious practices – Shachar's (2008) helpful example is that of a Jewish woman who obtained a divorce by state civil court but could not remarry and start a new life because her ex-husband did not allow her to obtain the religious divorce. According to Shachar, omissions and shortcomings could be circumvented by promoting the type of recognition close to the one which Woodman labels 'normative'.

As stated above, normative recognition consists in recognizing a sub-state normative ordering so that, in certain circumstances, its rules may be applied by state institutions in lieu of state legal rules. In his thoughtful analysis of the difficulties and potentialities of this recognition regime, Woodman (2008: 33–37) clarifies that many problems are likely to arise as state institutions put this model in practice. To mention but a few of them, state institutions would find themselves interpreting and enforcing rules that have been developed in different socio-cultural settings and reflect different values; they may be scarcely knowledgeable about the rules and principles of the recognized normative ordering and may lack reliable guidance. Moreover, in multicultural societies individuals involved in a particular case might abide at one and the same time by a multiplicity of orderings, so much so that it might be complicated to determine what normative repertoire should apply to the specific case. A similar train of thought leads Shachar (2012) to imagine a more flexible interplay between the recognizing law and the recognized ordering, one that makes room for negotiation within the dispute and escapes the risk of the Balkanization of justice. She espouses a case-by-case, piecemeal approach whereby state institutions permit the admission of cultural and/or religious variables as *relevant* considerations in settling disputes.

The idea that within state courts there should be a constant negotiation between state law and non-state orderings builds on an important intuition that permeated legal pluralism from the very beginning (Galanter 1981, 1983). Which is to say, the permeability of cultural narratives vis-à-vis the legal language in official dispute settlement contexts and, indirectly, even outside them. In this reading, any potential opposition or clash between frames of significance is tempered by the need for translation that I discussed at the outset of this book (see Introduction). 'The contribution of courts to resolving disputes cannot be equated with their resolution of those disputes that are fully adjudicated', as their principal contribution to dispute resolution 'is the provision of a background of norms and procedures against which negotiations and regulation in both private and governmental settings take place' (Galanter 1983: 121). This means that, well beyond the scope of the single dispute, the law lends itself as a space for an ongoing negotiation – however 'bounded' this negotiation may be. In the framework of normative recognition, the unpredictable interplay between official courts and normative orderings may transform the meaning and effects of both. In fact, when official courts are called upon to take into account the norms and principles of a given indigenous ordering, the effect is bilateral. On the one hand, official courts 'may radiate norms, symbols, models, threats, and so forth' (Galanter 1983: 132). On the other hand, members of sub-state groups engage in different forms of bargaining that they extract from the message conveyed by official courts – messages that can be given in single disputes, but then radiate all over other potential disputes – and transpose them into their own regulatory framework. This might be the way to face the challenge of legal pluralism that truly allows state law and legal pluralism to coexist.

There are many advantages to this approach. First, the challenge of pluralism – that, as I argued above, is particularly reflected in the qualifier 'legal' – is seriously taken up by state institutions, but in such a way that there are no penumbra zones where state law does not apply. Second, the issue of 'alternative' jurisdictions (whether or not religious-based) is by no means confined to the realm of the exotic and thus the private. As Shachar (2008) insists, this accommodates the concerns of vulnerable individuals precisely because it is made public and visible. The easy answer of limiting alternative justice to the private domain is but an 'out of sight, out of mind' approach that

> will probably not be of much assistance to vulnerable group members in blocking communal pressures to resolve family disputes by turning to 'their' group's authorities which, now legally unrecognized, remain free of any regulatory oversight, whether ex ante or ex post.
>
> (Shachar 2008: 605)

More importantly for my purposes, it does not simply reinstate a language that piggybacks on the legal lexicon. In fact, a vision of legal pluralism that aims at substituting a legal order for another, whether cultural- or religious-based, would be just as monist and monolithic as the state legal order. On the contrary, the continuous intercourse between normative contexts within a framework of normative recognition would empower law-users in an unprecedented manner, as the Conclusion of this book will try to illustrate. In the end, I believe this is the lesson we have to learn from the founding figures of legal pluralism. The state should cease to live on the fictitious idea of a common and homogenous legal framework able to identify the public good, which overrides all forms of sub-state normativity. At the same time, no social group could claim complete autonomy and replace state law for its internal ordering. This would make ample room for a politics of juridification that does not simply reinforce the law's clutch on the social but importantly introduces new bodies of law pivoting around law-users and the normativity arising from their daily activities.

Conclusion

1 As law-users make law

This book has explored such seemingly conflicting phenomena as the revision of sexual and kinship practices and the accommodation of non-state (mostly) religious-based normativities. These societal dynamics are believed to be at odds with one another as they raise opposite claims. While the demand for growing autonomy from state law advanced by religious sub-state groups is often justified with reference to principles like equality and fairness, this autonomy and its potential impact on state policies is accused of favouring a turn towards political conservatism, with detrimental effects on vulnerable subjects, both inside and outside those groups. In other words, the defence of religious habits and practices seems to be hardly reconcilable with the recognition of rights that unsettle traditional conceptions of sex and family, as ongoing outcries against same-sex marriage in many Western countries testify (see, for example, Cobb 2006; for an example of less vociferous, and yet resolute, oppositions to revisions of family law see Turner et al. 2017). Despite this, Chapters 1 and 2 were not concerned with the extension of sexual rights or the recognition of group autonomy as separate and isolable trajectories. Instead I intended to place these social struggles within the broader framework of the changing relation between law and politics. My analysis aimed at ferreting out the agential aspect of these phenomena with a view to investigating how and to what extent both LGB people and religious groups engage in a politics of juridification. In doing so, I tried to identify the transformative potential of something – like social agents' increasing recourse to legal means – that most often the critical literature associates with the unleashing of opaque governmental techniques. Therefore, against the *prima face* conflict between legislation on sexuality and legal pluralism, it is my conviction that reading the one against the background of the other corroborates the interpretation I have offered in the preceding chapters.

Elsewhere I contended that the (unexpected) intersection between these two phenomena could be conducive to a productive juridico-political development, which could be beneficial to liberal politics (see Croce 2015c). I embraced a legal-pluralist perspective to claim that such an irreconcilability could morph into a joint effort to break away from standard recognition strategies of liberal legal regimes mostly based on the jargon of rights (see Venditti 2016). My argument was that, within a genuinely post-secular setting (in the sense that I discussed in Section 2.1), legal pluralism could be a political weapon in the hands of LGB people because the pluralization of regulatory models could likely help them escape processes of normalization as they become authors of their own law. In the context of family law, legal pluralism could be one way to confront the 'selective legitimacy' of the state and its monopoly on the power to determine the types of relationships on which the state itself confers legality. In this reading, the conjunction of the issue of same-sex marriage and the plurality of legal regimes offers an example of how legal pluralism does not entail the erosion and dismissal of state legal orders. Quite the opposite, the introduction of legal pluralism in family law would reinvigorate them by facilitating the active involvement of law-users in the production of the relationship-recognition models that would be meant to regulate their conducts as members of different family assemblages.

This is a point developed compellingly by Jeffrey Redding (2010a, 2010b). He avers that the battle to gain access to traditional marriage may paradoxically prove disadvantageous to the LGB population. Along the lines of queer critiques of same-sex marriage, Redding (2014: 11) is convinced that mainstream LGB groups' case for equal marriage fosters 'regressive and hegemonic arguments – emphasizing the alleged importance of marriage for everyone, everywhere, and for all time'. To circumvent the sanctification of a conventional institution on the part of those who have long been banned from it, Redding claims LGB people should not so much pursue equality through marriage. Instead they should invoke autonomy in the construction of their own relationship-recognition regime. Commenting on contested California Proposition 8 – providing that 'only marriage between a man and a woman is valid or recognized in California' (which was ultimately ruled unconstitutional by a federal court in 2010, although the court decision only went into effect in 2013) – Redding argues for a strategic use of the unfair measures discriminating between traditional marriage and other forms of union. The asymmetry that these types of measures bring about could and should be set against the 'conventional (liberal) view' (Redding 2010a: 795) that equality entails an identical range of rights, benefits and responsibilities.

What concerns me in the context of this book is that Redding intentionally conjures what I call a politics of juridification as he invites LGB people – though in this case the acronym could be extended to cover transgender, queer, intersexual, asexual, pansexual people – to exercise agency with respect to the production of new pieces of family law legislation. Different relationship-recognition regimes would grant a set of benefits and rights tailored to the specific interests and needs of the people involved, with no conventional model of family prescribing the way in which rights and benefits should be allocated and enjoyed. Importantly, this use of the politics of juridification is able to reduce significantly the law's effects on that which is not directly addressed because it intentionally opens the door to imaginative, transformative uses of law. More precisely, using law in a pluralist sense avoids two risks: the oblique (see Introduction) effects of legal categorization that I unpacked in the first chapter; and the creation of penumbra zones that I touched upon at the end of the second chapter.

First, legal pluralism in family law curbs the oblique effects of legal categorization. As I tried to show throughout the book, the law's peculiar technique of description through official categories has performative effects not only on the social practices that categories designate and regulate, but also on those that are not directly affected. In the field of legal kinship (see Sections 1.2 and 1.3), legal categorization singles out a range of relationships to which the state grants recognition. Bourdieu's (1977: 33–37, 1990: 162–200) fine account of kinship brings out the normative power of the representation of official kinship – as a representation that is meant to prop up something through the power to speak on behalf of 'the public'. The authoritative description – one that always involves a prescription – of what kinship relations amount to makes certain relations socio-politically visible and speakable, and confines others to the realm of political (and to some extent social) inexistence (see also Swennen and Croce 2016). The active involvement of LGB individuals in the production of relationship-recognition regimes could eschew the normalization that comes with legal categorization. On the one hand, autonomous relationship-recognition regimes would not be modelled on already available, and hardly flexible, classifications and institutional structures. Such regimes would be the upshot of a creative process meant to produce new bodies of law, along with different norms, vocabularies and categories. On the other hand, the new classifications and institutional structures that would emerge out of this creative revision of state law would open the door to types of unions and family assemblages that exceed monogamous and life-long coupledom. In other words, the development of personal laws, meant to cover different types of situations expressing different needs and interests, would prompt law-users to design the rules that best meet such needs and interests. This approach would concretely move the debate beyond (straight and gay) marriage, so as to do away with the heterosexual matrix and the sticky speakability it offers lesbians, gay and bisexuals (see Polikoff 2008, where convincing arguments are advanced on the need to revise and extend the set of protections that marriage offers to many other types of unions and family assemblages). There is a second risk that this type of pluralism reduces, to wit, the creation of isolated, sealed off jurisdictions that make hierarchies and inequalities within groups. For there is no doubt that the adoption of a system whereby indigenous orderings would be straightforwardly endowed with legislative and administrative authority could jeopardize the position of vulnerable members and dissenters within sub-state groups. However, the politics of juridification that I am fleshing out would not pursue the aim of creating sub-state autonomous jurisdictions with distinctive authority on particular issues or sets of people. Rather, as I pointed out, it would bring about a scenario where LGB people (and people more generally as far as other issues that I have not tackled in this book are concerned) would be involved in the creation of distinctive pieces of common legislation. Certainly, involving people in the creation of law is far from easy. In the conclusive pages of this book I would like to outline two alternative routes that are both conducive to a legal pluralist scenario compatible with state legal orders. As I will discuss, both are modes of political juridification because law-users are active vehicles for the creation of pieces of legislation. What changes is the type of negotiation they engage in with the state.

2 Two modes of political juridification

The first mode of using law in such a way for people to be creators of their own family law regime is the introduction of personal laws, as recommended by Redding. I already pointed out that there is a crucial difference between a system of private orderings and a personal law system (Chapter 2, Section 2.2). The former entails a self-limitation by the state of its jurisdiction, as the state itself defines a set of issues which it leaves to the control of the sub-state group. People would then be put in the position of privately constructing alternatives to state family law, its rules and prescriptions. On the contrary, a personal law system is based on the inclusion within state law of provisions requiring its own institutions to give effect to the norms of different legal orderings – what corresponds to the model of 'normative recognition' described in Chapter 2, Section 2.2. In a personal law system, it is the state itself that is required to define and/or enforce different types of laws for different people. The state legal order makes room for discrete fragments of alternative orderings, whose rules state agencies would take it upon themselves to enforce. Such fragments of different legal bodies would reflect specific convictions, circumstances, needs and interests, and would apply to all those who believe that their particular situation requires legal regulation and protection. This type of pluralism in the field of family law would then give life to a state of different regimes granting different sets of benefits, rights and responsibilities differently relevant to different populations. The advantage of this system is that groups are not reified and constricted into crystallized units with essential features. For groups would not be given direct political-jurisdictional authority insofar as they would not be treated as reified, structured entities. Rather, it would be the process of normative recognition constructed along with the law-users that would require state law to include provisions comprising particular relationship-recognition regimes.

In effect, although mostly based on religious affiliation, personal laws that exist around the world are not static customary or scriptural normative bodies but the product of ongoing political negotiations and social struggles (see, for example, Basu 2003; Harel-Shalev 2013). At the same time, the path to legal unification and homogenization that in the last century was supposed to dispose of personal laws once and for all has proved at times politically ineffective or even detrimental to political stability or processes of democratization (see Künkler and Sezgin 2016). In the light of the renewal of religious agency of minority group members who try to bring about change 'from within', scholars provide evidence that intra-community struggles are a crucial engine of internal contestation and transformation (see, for example, the analysis of the rise of Muslim feminism reflected in the formation of women's groups in Vatuk 2001; Kirmani 2013; Harel-Shalev 2017). If applied to the Euro-American context, this solution is not so far from the 'menu-of-options' marriage system described by Janet Halley (2010: 33–36). It does result in a pluralization of models of unions as marriage – which becomes but one of the available options – ceases to be the quintessential model of union. Halley (2010: 39–44) discusses types of civil unions that allow greater contractual freedom. For example, covenant marriage in US states such as Arizona, Arkansas and Louisiana does seem to pluralize the family law system, as couples enjoy a broader capacity to contract at the beginning of marriage. A genuine pluralization could ensue from permitting people to engage in several forms at once, in such a way the 'menu-of-options plurality would resemble that on offer in the market, where players can elect between the corporate form, partnership, limited partnership, long-term contract, and so on, and can form relationships in which these forms overlap quite a bit' (Halley 2010: 43).

Not always, however, have personal laws or the 'menu-of-options' marriage system ended up promoting a genuine pluralization of the available legal framework. Halley notes that, despite initial expectations, most often this seeming pluralization contributed to reinforcing the idea of monogamy and restricted people to participate in only one form at a time. In other words, as illustrated by my discussion above of whether marriage is status or contract (see Chapter 1, Section 1.3) – which also built on Halley's (2011a; 2011b) refined analysis – family law policies have most often eventuated in a push-back that has enhanced the status character of the various new forms. This is why in these last few pages I would like to outline an alternative mode of recognition that hinges on a different politics of juridification. Needless to say, this topic would deserve a detailed analysis that I cannot offer here. However, it is worth briefly explaining what it is and why it looks more advantageous than a private law system.

This alternative mode of recognition is an approach that can be called 'cont(r)actualization' (see Swennen and Croce 2017). The bracketed '(r)' gestures towards a movement *from contact to contract*, as the *contacts* created by the members of a particular kinship assemblage are *legally contractualized* (on contractualization in family law, see Swennen 2015a and in particular Swennen 2015b). Cont(r)actualization intensifies law-users' ability to producer normativity of their own within interactional contexts and deactivates the circularity of the relation between legal kinship categories and people's claim to them examined in Chapter 1. In fact, it is a legal recognition strategy that pays heed to the connections created by social agents as they build up their kin formation. This means that, while recognizing the latter, legal institutions should leave aside predefined legal schemes that claim to define what social agents are doing and what they are in the eyes of one another. The law would be called upon to trace and account for the ways in which law-users get in touch with one another and create *points of contact*, and how they verbalize these contacts in ways that can be contractualized with recourse to a legal proxy.

To give an example relating to the recognition of family models, cont(r) actualization invites to dispose of the conventional family model that is incorporated in existing civil codes by desexualizing and pluralizing parental status. The latter need not be confined to one woman and one man, nor to persons who have a romantic relationship with each other, nor to two persons and not to (a) household(s) (recent governmental projects that work along these lines are mentioned in Swennen and Croce 2017). The basic idea is to substitute parenthood for interchangeable parental roles that could be labelled in a gender-neutral way (on the decertification of gender, see Cooper and Renz 2016; Katyal 2017), and thus abandon classical divisions such as mother/father, mother/co-mother and so on. Legislatures should provide for public civil registration of *all* potential family members. While registration is already an important means to obtain recognition, it does not need to go hand in hand with the attribution of a civil parental status. At the same time, though, it does not necessarily entail any hierarchies between the various figures of the family assemblage (e.g. a 'real' mother who is registered on the birth certificate, and other 'mothers' who are excluded from the birth register and thus from 'real' motherhood, and are relegated to 'the shadow' of registration in other – for example, donor or adoption – registers that confer some recognition but not a civil status).

On the other hand, this mode of recognition would not reduce the state to an inert observer who registers what people do. As discussed in Chapter 2, it behoves state institutions to make different normative contexts compatible as well as reconcile this scenario with its complex administrative and judicial machinery. One way in which the state might be involved in the passage from contact to contract is the delineation of a *modular system*. The state could/should allow distribution among multiple family figures of either all or some of the different kinship roles or functions within a formally fragmented parental status. For example, as far as parenthood is concerned, it could/should be split into *modules* that correspond to various functions, such as begetting/bearing, raising/nurturing/protecting, educating and endowing (see, for example, the functions singled out in Godelier 2012: 219–228). Within such a system, differentiation would be possible between the parents' significance for the (long-term) history and identity of a child. If, for instance, we apply this modular system to motherhood, the different women concerned can be accommodated in the begetter module (e.g. egg donor, mitochondrial donor), the nurturing module (e.g. intended woman), educating module (e.g. intended woman and symbolic presence for important decisions of the 'begetter') and/or endowing module (e.g. differentiated responsibilities for the women in the nurturing and educating modules respectively).

The legal-pluralist torsion of cont(r)actualization lies in the contention that decisions on the differentiation of parental roles and thus on the adoption of available modules should be made not by the state but by the actors themselves. On the one side, the availability of modules allows law-users to draw on institutional guidelines as they find themselves determining the content of their relations with the other family members. On the other side, modules are much less constricting than present-day family law categories as they pre-dispose legally regulated patterns of interaction. Predefined modules would thus enable law-users to flexibly re-model their family lives through active deliberation and innovation and through their application to new situations. In short, the cont(r)actual mode is a legal framework where law-users would have a central role to play in rethinking family law, as well as other bodies of law, and adapting them to the concrete practices people perform in everyday life.

3 The political potential of legal creativity

What matters for my purposes in this book is the political potential of cont(r) actualization. It is relevant to juridification in that it goes beyond the traditional divide between the public and the private as it gives rise to a web of juridified (private) legal transactions that lay claim to (public) legal validity. To make this point, I would like to introduce Santi Romano's view as he builds on his compelling institutional theory of legal pluralism to put forward an insightful account of 'autonomy'. Romano does not refer to the liberal conception of autonomy as the bordered sphere of individual will, separate from the public, and sheltered by individual rights. Rather, in his last book, *Frammenti di un dizionario giuridico* (*Fragments of a Legal Dictionary*), published in 1946, he locates his discussion of such an important notion within his legal-pluralist theoretical framework. He brings into question state law's tendency to qualify as 'non-legal', 'extra-legal' or 'a-legal' all that it does not qualify as 'legal' or 'illegal'. Indeed, from the point of view of state law 'all the other orders are claimed not to have . . . the characteristic of legality', as they are reduced to 'mere facts' (Romano [1946]1983: 19; all translations from this book are mine). By doing so, Romano brushes off the conventional bifurcation of the public as the realm of the common legislation and the private as the realm of individual autonomy. The fact that the latter is regarded as the source of private acts of will that seek legal recognition and enforcement is but a further instantiation of the monist mental habit that Romano denounces. He thus invites us to regard autonomy as a genuine source of valid law, because, *pace* Savigny, legal transactions between individuals do not only produce legal relationships but also issue norms. The latter are context-specific normative guidelines that respond to context-specific needs and interests. Romano concludes by saying that

> the specific characteristic of autonomy is to be found not in the will that it materializes, but in the objective fact of forming an order that has particular features of independence and, at the same time, dependence, that is to say, of limited independence from another order.
>
> (Romano [1946]1983: 29)

Romano deftly captures the fundamental characteristics of autonomous legal transactions: they are independent as far as their source of validity is concerned, while they are dependent in that they do not give life to a fully-fledged order. This also means that law does not only depend on there being a complete and self-standing system. The normative structure of legal transactions, pivoted on social agents' autonomy, is in fact semi-autonomous. Romano gestures to a law that has no firm structure and borders, and certainly does not easily comply with territorial coordinates or limits. The law is a *point of view*. Or better, a juristic point of view from which reality can be reframed through the prism of law in order to exert particular effects on reality (see Croce 2017b). Unlike Yan Thomas' account (1995, 2004), however, Romano's conception makes room for a notion of the legal order as a plurality of semi-autonomous legal fragments that helps lessen the obliquity of specialized legal techniques. In short, while Romano sides with Thomas when it comes to the descriptive force of law, he insists that law can hardly give up the contribution of other (non-state; in Romano's view genuinely legal) entities to give shape to the legal order. If the state disposes of its innate inclination to posit an equivalence between state law and the law as such, then the juristic point of view can finally attend to what it is called upon to do.

What is it that it is called upon to do, then? An answer that I believe provides the key to many of the problems analyzed in this book is: to work through the fine line that exists between describing things and regulating them obliquely. As Maurizio Fioravanti (1981: 217) comments, Romano's claim is that (what I call) describing reality through the prism of law helps realize that 'there is no contradiction between the new socio-political pluralism and the basic characteristics of the modern state'. For what I call the 'juristic point of view' (Croce 2017b) illustrates that 'no system of public law is conceivable as a complete and coherent whole that makes no room for "society" as an indirectly productive source of continuous integrations to the legal order' (Fioravanti 1981: 218). In other words, if it is true that the law is a powerful, consequence-laden descriptive technique, it is just as true that it can be used as a point of view where social agents can constantly reframe, redescribe, rethink their interactions. Romano's foremost insight is that the law does not need to provide substantive contents, because the sources of valid law are countless. In this sense, autonomous legal transactions in Romano's lexicon stand as forms of contacts among social agents that can be rendered into contracts as they enter the official legal field to be described in legal terms. At the same time, this description need not be based on a pre-given vocabulary, modelled on existing forms of life or regulatory frameworks, because legal transactions, based on social agents' autonomy, are in principle capable of creating an infinity of new vocabularies. This is the key to a politics of juridification that I deem to be all but depoliticizing and normalizing.

Needless to say, hardly ever can the descriptive technique of the law give up its constitutive claim to be grounded on anything but its own knowledge and categories. And yet, as Romano's overall conception seems to suggest, this knowledge and these categories can at any moment be put to work to engender a revision of state law in the sense of its compatibility with other forms of normativity and the conceptual frameworks these forms pivot around. To put it another way, the law's alleged autonomy and self-sufficiency can be used to open up spaces for law-users to construct new fragments of law. This openness to remain open is what counteracts law's inborn obliquity. And this is the characteristic – which importantly in Romano's view is a distinguishing mark of law, one that monist conceptions of the legal order most often neglect – that enables a transformative use of the politics of juridification. In this frame, juridification inhibits the spiral of normalization because law-users are called upon to play a creative role, based on the practical activities they carry out on a daily basis. The law would only serve as a juristic point of view whence law-users, under the guidance of professionals, can account for what they are and do with an eye to producing a legal description of their normative context. It goes without saying that a transformation/alteration of these contexts is inevitable. As Woodman comments as he discusses normative recognition, the latter

> often entails the application and enforcement within the recognising law of a body of norms which has been developed in a different social and legal environment and reflects different values. A simple, direct adoption of these norms into the legal environment of the recognising law is rarely possible.
>
> (Woodman 2008: 34)

While Woodman has in mind the multiple relations between state law and customary (mostly religious) orderings, his observation is certainly also relevant to the notion of cont(r)actualization. What people do in the context of their normative frameworks, whether greater or smaller, does not easily translate into the legal order in unchanged forms. In effect, as I pointed out at the very beginning of this book, law is an 'as if' that constitutively moves away from facts as a possibility condition for it to operate on facts. Legal conversion always entails various processes of stabilization, generalization and formalization. But insofar as the law lets its fissures be infiltrated by the creativity of law-users, the oblique effects it exerts on that which is not directly addressed are likely to be less pervasive. The autonomy of law-users arises as a new way – neither private nor public – to make the legal order fit the normativity of everyday life, while the juristic point of view prevents the fractalization or even the Balkanization of the social world. Yet the interplay between identity and difference that feeds legal pluralism cannot be the identity and difference of objectivity and substance. Romano's conception entails a view of entities that hardly stay the same as they engage in various forms of negotiation. As the law is not a thing or an object, but a point of view, so are the various normative contexts that it gets in touch with. Accordingly, what I want to get at is not that cont(r)actualization simply portrays and stabilizes contacts within family assemblages or religious or cultural groups *as they are* because there *is no stable being*. The politics of juridification – the one that I champion in this book – inevitably entails internal transition and transvaluation.

This explains why I insisted on the difference between personal laws and cont(r)actualization. The latter is a gesture to the irreducible multiplicity of being that can never be simply recognized and categorized. For a web of contacts can never be congealed into a static model. The juristic point of view serves as a descriptor in the hands of law-users – social agents that have recourse to law – when they need modular guidelines to predict the (often unpredictable) effects of their movements within their interactional contexts. In the end, the legal-pluralist view that orients cont(r)actualization dovetails with Eduardo Viveiros de Castro's notion of 'multiplicity', which can never be

an essence. The dimensions composing it are neither constitutive properties nor criteria for classificatory inclusion. A chief component of the concept of multiplicity is, on the contrary, the notion of individuation as non-taxonomical differentiation; the process of the actualization of a virtual different from the realization of the possible through limitation and refractory to the typological categories of similitude, opposition, analogy, and identity.

(Viveiros de Castro 2014: 109)

The politics of juridification by which law-users have recourse to law to have their contacts contractualized is not meant to instantiate a generalizable type. Rather, a cont(r)actualized assemblage 'is an acentric reticular system constituted by intensive relations ("becomings") between heterogeneous singularities that correspond to events, or extrasubstantive individuations ("haecceities")' (Viveiros de Castro 2014: 109). After all, the incongruities between the ontologies and epistemologies Romano and Viveiros de Castro work with are negligible when Romano ([1946]1983: 205) pithily describes the law as a mediatory (see Latour 2005: 37–42) activity of assemblage:

A state, a Church, an international company, a family, any social organization whatsoever are nothing but legal entities: the law certainly does not create them from nothingness, but, by assembling, gathering together, and ordering the various elements that they are comprised of, give real and effective life within the legal world to entities that cannot be confused or identified with any of those elements.

(Romano [1946]1983: 205)

The intercourse between the activity of law-users and the law they use to provide an account that has legal effects transforms both this activity and the law. Insofar as the law gets rid of pre-constituted models and their oblique effects, this intercourse is likely to be conducive to countless legal forms that feed off the imagination and creativity of those who are involved in them. The law can still play an important role to make sure that the position of weak and vulnerable people is not worsened, but in a way that is respectful of the normative life of the cont(r)actualized assemblages. If the law ceases to foster the 'homogenisation of ideas of what is acceptable in ways of governing, what are legitimate expectations between the governing and the governed and what are breaches of norms' (Eckert 2006: 70) that should guide opposition and resistance, the politics of juridification will serve as a precious transformative means – one that does not ingenuously present the law as a mere form of domination and at the same time make its semiotic territory hospitable to people who aim to do things in ways that may not conform with conventional social models and existing legal schemes.

Bibliography

Ammerman, N. (1997) 'Organized Religion in a Voluntaristic Society', *Sociology of Religion* 58: 203–215.

Andersen, M.L. (1991) 'Feminism and the American Family Ideal', *Journal of Comparative Family Studies* 22(2): 235–246.

Asad, T. (2003) *Formations of the Secular: Christianity, Islam, Modernity*, Stanford, CA: Stanford University Press.

Aune, K. (2015) 'Feminist Spirituality as Lived Religion. How UK Feminists Forge Religio-spiritual Lives', *Gender & Society* 29(1): 122–145.

Bader, V. (2012) '"Post-Secularism" or Liberal-Democratic Constitutionalism?', *Erasmus Law Review* 5: 5–26.

Bailey, T., Gentile, V. (eds) (2014) *Rawls and Religion*, New York: Columbia University Press.

Ball, C.A. (2009) 'Symposium: Updating the LGBT Intracommunity Debate over Same-sex Marriage. Introduction', *Rutgers Law Review* 61: 493–505.

Bano, S. (2008) 'In Pursuit of Religious and Legal Diversity: A Response to the Archbishop of Canterbury and the "Sharia Debate" in Britain', *Ecclesiastical Law Journal* 10: 283–309.

Barker, M., Langdridge, D. (2010) 'Whatever Happened to Non-monogamies? Critical Reflections on Recent Research and Theory', *Sexualities* 13(6): 748–772.

Barrett, M., McIntosh, M. (1982) *The Anti-Social Family*, London: Verso.

Barzilai, G. (2007) 'The Ambivalent Language of Lawyers in Israel: Liberal Politics, Economic Liberalism, Silence and Dissent', in Halliday, T.C., Karpik, L., Feeley, M. (eds), *Fighting for Political Freedom: Comparative Studies of the Legal Complex and Political Liberalism*, Oxford and Portland, OR: Hart Publishing, pp. 247–277.

Basu, S. (2003) 'Shading the Secular. Law at Work in the Indian Higher Courts', *Cultural Dynamics* 15(2): 131–152.

Beckford, J.A. (2012) 'Public Religions and the Postsecular: Critical Reflections', *Journal for the Scientific Study of Religion* 51: 1–19.

Beiner, R. (2011) *Civil Religion. A Dialogue in the History of Political Philosophy*, Cambridge: Cambridge University Press.

Bellow, G. (1996) 'Steady Work: A Practitioner's Reflections on Political Lawyering', *Harvard Civil Rights-Civil Liberties Law Review* 31: 297–309.

Berger, P.L. (1998) 'Protestantism and the Quest of Certainty', *The Christian Century* 2: 782–796.

Berman, P.S. (2007) 'Global Legal Pluralism', *Southern California Review* 80: 1155–1237.

Bleier, R. (1984) *Science and Gender: A Critique of Biology and Its Themes on Women*, New York: Pergamon.

Blichner, L.C., Molander, A. (2008) 'Mapping Juridification', *European Law Journal* 14: 36–54.

Böckenförde, E.-W. (1991) *State, Society, and Liberty: Studies in Political Theory and Constitutional Law*, New York and Oxford: Berg.

Bourdieu, P. (1985) 'The Social Space and the Genesis of Groups', *Theory and Society* 14(6): 723–744.

Bourdieu, P. (1987) 'The Force of Law: Toward a Sociology of the Juridical Field', *Hastings Law Journal* 38: 814–853.

Bourdieu, P. (1990) *The Logic of Practice*, Stanford, CA: Stanford University Press.

Bourdieu, P. (1991) *Language and Symbolic Power*, Cambridge: Polity.

Bourdieu, P. (2001) *Masculine Domination*, Stanford, CA: Stanford University Press.

Bracke, S. (2008) 'Conjugating the Modern/Religious, Conceptualizing Female Religious Agency: Contours of a "Post-secular" Conjuncture', *Theory, Culture & Society* 25(6): 51–75.

Braidotti, R. (2008) 'In Spite of the Times. The Postsecular Turn in Feminism', *Theory, Culture & Society* 25(6): 1–24.

Bunch, C. (1987) *Passionate Politics: Feminist Theory in Action*, New York: St. Martin's Press.

Burden and Burden v. the United Kingdom (2008) European Court of Human Rights, 29 April, available at http://hudoc.echr.coe.int/sites/eng/pages/search. aspx?i=001-86146.

Butler, J. (1997) *Excitable Speech: A Politics of the Performative*, London: Routledge.

Butler, J. (2004) *Undoing Gender*, New York: Routledge.

Caputo, J.D. (2001) *On Religion*, London and New York: Routledge.

Carsten, J. (2000) *Cultures of Relatedness: New Approaches to the Study of Kinship*, Cambridge: Cambridge University Press.

Casanova, J. (2006) 'Rethinking Secularization: A Global Comparative Perspective', *Hedgehog Review* 8: 7–22.

Casanova, J. (2009) 'The Secular and Secularisms', *Social Research* 76: 1149–1166.

Cobb, M. (2006) *God Hates Fags: The Rhetorics of Religious Violence*, New York: New York University Press.

Collier, J.F., Yanagisako, S.J. (eds) (1987) *Gender and Kinship: Essays Towards a Unified Analysis*, Stanford, CA: Stanford University Press.

Collins, P.H. (2001) 'Like One of the Family: Race, Ethnicity, and the Paradox of US National Identity', *Ethnic and Racial Studies* 24(1): 3–28.

Comaroff, J.L. (2009) 'Reflections on the Rise of Legal Theology: Law and Religion in the Twenty-first Century', *Social Analysis* 53(1): 193–216.

Comaroff, J., Comaroff, J.L. (2006) 'Law and Disorder in the Postcolony: An Introduction', in Comaroff, J., Comaroff, J.L. (eds), *Law and Disorder in the Postcolony*, Chicago, IL: The University of Chicago Press, pp. 1–56.

Comaroff, J., Comaroff, J.L. (2009) 'Reflections on the Anthropology of Law, Governance and Sovereignty', in von Benda-Beckmann, F., von Benda-Beckmann, K., Eckert (eds), *Rules of Law and Law of Ruling*, Farnham: Ashgate, pp. 31–59.

Comaroff, J.L., Roberts, S. (1981) *Rules and Processes. The Cultural Logic of Dispute in an African Context*, Chicago, IL: The University of Chicago Press.

Cooper, D. (2001) 'Like Counting Stars? Re-Structuring Equality and the Socio-Legal Space of Same-sex Marriage', in Wintemute, R., Andenæs, M.T. (eds), *Legal Recognition of Same-sex Partnerships: A Study of National, European and International Law*, Oxford and Portland, OR: Hart Publishing, pp. 75–96.

Cooper, D. (2014) *Everyday Utopias: The Conceptual Life of Promising Spaces*, Durham, NC, and London: Duke University Press.

Cooper, D., Renz, F. (2016) 'If the State Decertified Gender, What Might Happen to its Meaning and Value?', *Journal of Law and Society* 43(4): 483–505.

Croce, M. (2012) *Self-Sufficiency of Law. A Critical-Institutional Theory of Social Order*, Dordrecht: Springer.

Croce, M. (2014) 'Is Law a Special Domain? On the Boundary Between the Legal and the Social', in Donlan, S.P., Heckerdorn-Urscheler, L. (eds), *Concepts of Law: Comparative, Jurisprudential, and Social Science Perspectives*, Farnham: Ashgate, pp. 153–167.

Croce, M. (2015a) 'Governing Through Normality: Law and the Force of Sameness', *International Journal of Politics, Culture and Society* 28(4): 303–323.

Croce, M. (2015b) 'From Gay Liberation to Marriage Equality: A Political Lesson to be Learnt', *European Journal of Political Theory*, published online before print 16 April 2015, DOI: 10.1177/1474885115581425.

Croce, M. (2015c) 'Secularization, Legal Pluralism and the Question of Relationship-Recognition Regimes', *The European Legacy* 20(2): 151–165.

Croce, M. (2017a) 'The Enemy as the Unthinkable: A Concretist Reading of Carl Schmitt's Conception of the Political', *History of European Ideas*, published online 8 February 2017, DOI: http://dx.doi.org/10.1080/01916599.2017.1285099.

Croce, M. (2017b) 'The Juristic Point of View: An Interpretive Account of *The Legal Order*', in Romano, S., *The Legal Order*, Abingdon, UK: Routledge, pp. 110–127.

Croce, M., Goldoni, M. (2015) 'A Sense of Self-suspicion: Global Legal Pluralism and the Claim to Legal Authority', *Ethics & Global Politics* 8(1): 1–20.

Croce, M., Salvatore, A. (2013) *The Legal Theory of Carl Schmitt*, Abingdon, UK: Routledge.

Croce, M., Salvatore, A. (2017) 'Normality as Social Semantics. Schmitt, Bourdieu and the Politics of the Normal', *European Journal of Social Theory* 20(2): 275–291.

Cussins, C. (1998) 'Producing Reproduction: Techniques of Normalization and Naturalization in Infertility Clinics', in Franklin, S., Ragoné, H. (eds), *Reproducing Reproduction: Kinship, Power, Technological Innovation*, Philadelphia, PA: University of Pennsylvania Press, pp. 66–101.

Dalferth, I.U. (2010) 'Post-Secular Society: Christianity and the Dialectics of the Secular', *Journal of the American Academy of Religion* 78: 317–345.

Daum, C.W. (2017) 'Marriage Equality: Assimilationist Victory or Pluralist Defeat?', in Burgess, S., Brettschneider, M., Keating, C. (eds), *LGBTQ Politics: A Critical Reader*, New York: New York University Press, pp. 353–373.

De Vries, H., Sullivan, L.E. (eds) (2006) *Political Theologies: Public Religions in a Post-secular World*, Bronx, NY: Fordham University Press.

Dempsey, D. (2010) 'Conceiving and Negotiating Reproductive Relationships', *Sociology* 44(6): 1145–1162.

Diduck, A. (2007) '"If Only We Can Find the Appropriate Terms to Use the Issue Will Be Solved": Law, Identity and Parenthood', *Child and Family Law Quarterly* 19(4): 458–480.

Eckert, J. (2006) 'From Subjects to Citizens: Legalism from Below and the Homogenisation of the Legal Sphere', *Journal of Legal Pluralism and Unofficial Law* 53–54: 45–75.

Edwards, J., Franklin, S., Hirsch, E., Price, F., Strathern, M. (eds) (1999) *Technologies of Procreation: Kinship in the Age of Assisted Conception*, London: Routledge.

Eekelaar, J. (2009) *Family Law and Personal Life*, Oxford: Oxford University Press.

Eekelaar, J. (2012) 'Self-Restraint: Social Norms, Individualism and the Family', *Theoretical Inquiries in Law* 13(1): 75–95.

Ehrlich, E. (2009) *Fundamental Principles of the Sociology of Law*, New Brunswick, NJ: Transaction Publishers.

Emens, E.F. (2004) 'Monogamy's Law: Compulsory Monogamy and Polyamorous Existence', *NYU Review of Law & Social Change* 29: 277–376.

Eskridge, W.N. (2013) 'Backlash Politics: How Constitutional Litigation Has Advanced Marriage Equality in the United States', *Boston University Law Review* 93: 275–323.

Ettelbrick, P.L. (1989) 'Since When Is Marriage a Path to Liberation?', *Out/look: National Lesbian and Gay Quarterly* 6: 14–16.

Fausto-Sterling, A. (1985) *Myths of Gender: Biological Theories about Men and Women*, New York: Basic Books.

Fausto-Sterling, A. (2012)*Sex/Gender: Biology in a Social World*, New York: Routledge.

Ferrara, A. (2009) 'The Separation of Religion and Politics in a Post-secular Society', *Philosophy and Social Criticism* 35: 77–91.

Finn, M., Malson, H. (2008) 'Speaking of Home Truth: (Re)Productions of Dyadic-Containment in Non-monogamous Relationships', *British Journal of Social Psychology* 47(3): 519–533.

Fioravanti, M. (1981) 'Per l'interpretazione dell'opera giuridica di Santi Romano', *Quaderni fiorentini per la storia del pensiero giuridico moderno* 10: 169–219.

Forsyth, C. (ed.) (2000) *Judicial Review and the Constitution*, Oxford and Portland, OR: Hart.

Foucault, M. (1978) *History of Sexuality, I: An Introduction*, New York: Pantheon Books.

Franklin, S. (2013) *Biological Relatives: IVF, Stem Cells, and the Future of Kinship*, Durham, NC, and London: Duke University Press.

Franklin, S., McKinnon, S. (eds) (2012) *Relative Values: Reconfiguring Kinship Studies*, Durham, NC: Duke University Press.

Friedan, B. (1998) *The Second Stage*, Cambridge, MA: Harvard University Press.

Galanter, M. (1981) 'Justice in Many Rooms: Courts, Private Ordering, and Indigenous Law', *Journal of Legal Pluralism and Unofficial Law* 19: 1–47.

Galanter, M. (1983) 'The Radiating Effects of Courts', in Boyum, K.D., Mather, L. (eds), *Empirical Theories about Courts*, New York: Longman, pp. 117–142.

Gay Liberation Front ([1973]1978) *Manifesto*, London.

Godelier, M. (2012) *The Metamorphoses of Kinship*, London: Verso.

Green, A.I. (2007) 'Queer Theory and Sociology: Locating the Subject and the Self in Sexuality Studies', *Sociological Theory* 25(1): 26–45.

Greenhouse, C.J. (1998) 'Legal Pluralism and Cultural Difference. What Is the Difference? A Response to Professor Woodman', *Journal of Legal Pluralism and Unofficial Law* 42: 61–72.

Griffiths, J. (1986) 'What Is Legal Pluralism?', *Journal of Legal Pluralism and Unofficial Law* 24: 1–55.

Grossi, P. (2010) *A History of European Law*, Malden, MA: Blackwell Publishing.

Habermas, J. (2006) 'On the Relations Between the Secular Liberal State and Religion', in De Vries, Sullivan, H. (eds), *Political Theologies. Public Religions in a Post-secular World*, New York: Fordham University Press, pp. 251–260.

Habermas, J. (2010) 'An Awareness of What Is Missing', in Habermas, J. (ed), *An Awareness of What Is Missing. Faith and Reason in a Post-secular Age*, Cambridge: Polity Press, pp. 15–23.

Hacking, I. (1996) 'The Looping Effects of Human Kinds', in Sperber, D., Premack, D., Premack, A.J. (eds), *Causal Cognition: A Multidisciplinary Debate*, Oxford: Oxford University Press, pp. 351–394.

Halley, J. (2010) 'Behind the Law of Marriage (I)', *Unbound* 6(1): 1–58.

Halley, J. (2011a) 'What Is Family Law?: A Genealogy. Part I', *Yale Journal of Law & the Humanities* 23: 1–109.

Halley, J. (2011b) 'What Is Family Law?: A Genealogy. Part II', *Yale Journal of Law & the Humanities* 23: 189–293.

Halperin, D.M. (2002) *How to Do the History of Homosexuality*, Chicago, IL:The University of Chicago Press.

Hamer, D., Copeland, P. (1994) *The Science of Desire. The Search for the Gay Gene and the Biology of Behaviour*, New York: Simon and Schuster.

Hammack, P.L., Cohler, B.J. (2009) *The Story of Sexual Identity. Narrative Perspectives on the Gay and Lesbian Life Course*, Oxford: Oxford University Press.

Harel-Shalev, A. (2013) 'Policy Analysis beyond Personal Law: Muslim Women's Rights in India', *Politics & Policy* 41(3): 384–419.

Harel-Shalev, A. (2017) 'Gendering Ethnic Conflicts: Minority Women in Divided Societies – The Case of Muslim Women in India', *Ethnic and Racial Studies* 40(12): 2115–2134.

Haritaworn, J., Lin, C.j., Klesse, C. (2006) 'Poly/logue: A Critical Introduction to Polyamory', *Sexualities* 9(5): 515–529.

Hayden, C.P. (1995) 'Gender, Genetics, and Generation: Reformulating Biology in Lesbian Kinship', *Cultural Anthropology* 10: 41–63.

Herman, D. (1990) 'Are We Family?: Lesbian Rights and Women's Liberation', *Osgoode Hall Law Journal* 28: 789–815.

Hertogh, M., Halliday S. (eds) (2004) *Judicial Review and Bureaucratic Impact: International and Interdisciplinary Perspectives*, Cambridge: Cambridge University Press.

Hirschl, R. (2004) *Towards Juristocracy: The Origins and Consequences of the New Constitutionalism*, Cambridge, MA: Harvard University Press.

Hirschl, R. (2006) 'The New Constitutionalism and the Judicialization of Pure Politics Worldwide', *Fordham Law Review* 75(2): 721–754.

Hirschl, R. (2008) 'The Judicialization of Politics', in Caldeira, G.A., Kelemen, R.D., Whittington, K.E. (eds), *The Oxford Handbook of Law and Politics*, Oxford: Oxford University Press, pp. 119–141.

Hirschl, R., Shachar, A. (2009) 'The New Wall of Separation: Permitting Diversity, Restricting Competition', *Cardozo Law Review* 30: 2535–2560.

Honig, B. (2009) *Emergency Politics: Paradox, Law, Democracy*, Princeton, NJ: Princeton University Press.

Joshi, Y. (2012) 'Respectable Queerness', *Columbia Human Rights Law Review* 43(2): 415–467.

Katyal, S.K. (2017) 'The Numerus Clausus of Sex', *University of Chicago Law Review* 84: 389–494.

Keller, E.F. (1995) 'Gender and Science: Origin, History, and Politics', *Osiris* 10 (2nd Series): 26–38.

Kirmani, N. (2013) *Questioning the 'Muslim Woman': Identity and Insecurity in an Urban Indian Locality*, Abingdon, UK: Routledge.

Klesse, C. (2007) *The Spectre of Promiscuity: Gay Male and Bisexual Non-monogamies and Polyamories*, Aldershot: Ashgate.

Klesse, C. (2014) 'Polyamory: Intimate Practice, Identity or Sexual Orientation?', *Sexualities* 17(1/2) 81–99.

Künkler, M., Sezgin, Y. (2016) 'The Unification of Law and the Postcolonial State: The Limits of State Monism in India and Indonesia', *American Behavioral Scientist* 60(8): 987–1012.

Kymlicka, W. (1991) 'Rethinking the Family', *Philosophy & Public Affairs* 20(1): 77–97.

Latour, B. (2005) *Reassembling the Social: An Introduction to Actor-Network-Theory*, Oxford: Oxford University Press.

Latour, B. (2013) *An Inquiry into Modes of Existence. An Anthropology of the Moderns*, Cambridge, MA: Harvard University Press.

Lawrence v. Texas, 123 S. Ct. 2472, 539 U.S., Opinion of the Court, Oral Argument Transcript.

Leckey, R. (2013) 'Two Mothers in Law and Fact', *Feminist Legal Studies* 21(1): 1–19.

Leming, L.M. (2007) 'Sociological Explorations: What Is Religious Agency?', *The Sociological Quarterly* 48: 73–92.

Lessard, H. (2004) 'Mothers, Fathers and Naming: Reflections on the Law Equality Framework and *Trociuk v British Columbia (Attorney General)*', *Canadian Journal of Women and the Law* 16: 165–211.

Lloyd, M. (2007) 'Radical Democratic Activism and the Politics of Resignification', *Constellations* 14(1): 129–46.

Löfström, J. (1997) 'The Birth of the Queen/the Modern Homosexual: Historical Explanations Revisited', *The Sociological Review* 45(1): 24–41.

Magnussen, A.-M., Banasiak, A. (2013) 'Juridification: Disrupting the Relationship between Law and Politics?', *European Law Journal*, 19(3): 325–339.

Mahmood, S. (2005) *Politics of Piety: The Islamic Revival and the Feminist Subject*, Princeton, NJ: Princeton University Press.

McGee, K. (2015) 'The Fragile Force of Law: Mediation, Stratification, and Law's Material Life', *Law, Culture and the Humanities* 11(3): 467–490.

Melissaris, E., Croce, M. (2017) 'A Pluralism of Legal Pluralisms', *Oxford Handbooks Online*, DOI: 10.1093/oxfordhb/9780199935352.013.22.

Menski, W. (2010a) 'Sanskrit Law: Excavating Vedic Legal Pluralism', *SOAS School of Law Legal Studies Research Paper* 5: 1–44.

Menski, W. (2010b) 'Beyond Europe', in Örücü, E., Nelken, D. (eds), *Comparative Law*, Oxford and Portland, OR: Hart, pp. 189–216.

Menski, W. (2011) 'Islamic Law in British Courts: Do We Not Know or Do We Not Want to Know?', in Mair, J., Örücü, E. (eds), *The Place of Religion in Family Law: A Comparative Search*, Mortsel: Intersentia, pp. 15–36.

Nader, L. (1984) 'A User Theory of Law', *Southwestern Law Journal* 38: 951–964.

Nader, L. (2002) *The Life of the Law*, Berkeley, CA: University of California Press.

NeJaime, D. (2003) 'Marriage, Cruising, and Life In Between: Clarifying Organizational Positionalities in Pursuit of Polyvocal Gay-Based Advocacy', *Harvard Civil Rights-Civil Liberties Law Review* 38: 512–562.

O'Brien, J. (2004) 'Wrestling the Angel of Contradiction: Queer Christian Identities', *Culture and Religion* 5(2): 179–202.

Okin, S.M. (1989) *Justice, Gender, and the Family*, New York: Basic Books.

Pakulski, J. (2014) 'Confusions about Multiculturalism', *Journal of Sociology* 50(1): 23–36.

Pilecki, A., Hammack, P.L. (2015) 'Invoking "The Family" to Legitimize Gender- and Sexuality-based Public Policies in the United States: A Critical Discourse Analysis of the 2012 Democratic and Republican National Party Conventions', *Journal of Social and Political Psychology* 3(1): 8–23.

Polikoff, N.D. (2008) *Beyond (Straight and Gay) Marriage: Valuing All Families under the Law*, Boston, MA: Beacon Press.

Puar, J. (2013) 'Homonationalism as Assemblage: Viral Travels, Affective Sexualities', *Jindal Global Law Review* 4(2): 23–43.

Ragoné, H. (1994) *Surrogate Motherhood: Conception in the Heart*, Boulder, CO: Westview Press.

Rawls, J. (2005) *Political Liberalism*, expanded edition, New York: Columbia University Press.

Red Collective ([1973]1978) *The Politics of Sexuality in Capitalism*, London: Red Collective/Publications Distribution Cooperative.

Redding, J.A. (2007) 'Slicing the American Pie: Federalism and Personal Law', *NYU Journal of International Law and Politics* 40(4): 941–1018.

Redding, J.A. (2010a) 'Dignity, Legal Pluralism, and Same-sex Marriage', *Brooklyn Law Review* 75: 791–863.

Redding, J.A. (2010b) 'Queer/Religious Friendship in the Obama Era', *Washington University Journal of Law & Policy* 33: 211–272.

Redding, J.A. (2014) 'Querying Edith Windsor, Querying Equality', *Villanova Law Review Online: Tolle Lege* 59: 9–16, available at http://digitalcommons.law.vil lanova.edu/cgi/viewcontent.cgi?article=3256&context=vlr.

Richardson, D. (2000) 'Constructing Sexual Citizenship. Theorizing Sexual Rights', *Critical Social Policy* 20(1) (2000):105–135.

Ritchie, A., Barker, M. (2006) '"There Aren't Words for What We Do or How We Feel so We Have to Make Them Up": Constructing Polyamorous Languages in a Culture of Compulsory Monogamy', *Sexualities* 9(5): 584–601.

Robertson, D. (2010) *The Judge as Political Theorist: Contemporary Constitutional Review*, Princeton, NJ: Princeton University Press.

Robinson, M. (2013) 'Polyamory and Monogamy as Strategic Identities', *Journal of Bisexuality* 13: 21–38.

Robinson, V. (1997) 'My Baby Just Cares for Me: Feminism, Heterosexuality and Non-monogamy', *Journal of Gender Studies* 6(2): 143–157.

Romano, S. ([1946]1983) *Frammenti di un dizionario giuridico*, Milano: Giuffrè.

Romano, S. (2017) *The Legal Order*, Abingdon, UK: Routledge.

Roy, O. (2007) *Secularism Confronts Islam*, New York: Columbia University Press.

Runciman, D. (1997) *Pluralism and the Personality of the State*, Cambridge: Cambridge University Press.

Ruskola, T. (2005) 'Gay Rights versus Queer Theory', *Social Text* 23(3–4): 235–249.

Schmitt, C. ([1930]2000) 'State Ethics and the Pluralist State', in Jacobson, A.J., Schlink, B. (eds), *Weimar. A Jurisprudence of Crisis*, Berkeley and Los Angeles, CA: University of California Press, pp. 300–312.

Schneider, D.M. (1980) *American Kinship. A Cultural Account*, Chicago, IL: University of Chicago Press, 2nd ed.

Schneider, D.M. (1984) *A Critique of the Study of Kinship*, Ann Arbor, MI: University of Michigan Press.

Schneider, D.M. (1997) 'The Power of Culture: Notes on Some Aspects of Gay and Lesbian Kinship in America Today', *Cultural Anthropology* 12(2): 270–274.

Shachar, A. (2001) *Multicultural Jurisdictions: Cultural Differences and Women's Rights*, Cambridge: Cambridge University Press.

Shachar, A. (2008) 'Privatizing Diversity: A Cautionary Tale from Religious Arbitration in Family Law', *Theoretical Inquiries in Law* 9(2): 573–607.

Shachar, A. (2012) 'Demystifying Culture', *International Journal of Constitutional Law* 10(2):429–448.

Shapiro M., Stone Sweet, A. (2002) *On Law, Politics, and Judicialization*, New York: Oxford University Press.

Shapiro, W. (2012) 'Anti-Family Fantasies in "Cutting-Edge" Anthropological Kinship Studies', *Academic Questions* 25(3): 394–402.

Sheff, E. (2011) 'Polyamorous Families, Same-sex Marriage, and the Slippery Slope', *Journal of Contemporary Ethnography* 40(5): 487–520.

Simpson, B. (1998) *Changing Families: An Ethnographic Approach to Divorce and Separation*, Oxford: Berg.

Smart, C. (1984) *The Ties that Bind: Law, Marriage and the Reproduction of Patriarchal Relations*, London: Routledge and Kegan Paul.

Soini, S., Ibarreta D., Anastasiadou V., Aymé S., Braga S., Cornel M. et al. (2006) 'The Interface between Assisted Reproductive Technologies and Genetics: Technical, Social, Ethical and Legal Issues', *European Journal of Human Genetics* 14: 588–645.

Spanier, B. (2005) 'Biological Determinism and Homosexuality', in Robertson, J. (ed.), *Same-sex Cultures and Sexualities: An Anthropological Reader*, Malden, MA: Blackwell Publishers, pp. 33–47.

Sparti, D. (2001) 'Making Up People: On Some Looping Effects of the Human Kind – Institutional Reflexivity or Social Control?', *European Journal of Social Theory* 4(3): 331–239.

Stein, E. (2009) 'Marriage or Liberation? Reflections on Two Strategies in the Struggle for Lesbian and Gay Rights and Relationship Recognition', *Rutgers Law Review* 61: 567–593.

Stoddard, T. (1989) 'Why Gay People Should Seek the Right to Marry', *Out/look: National Lesbian and Gay Quarterly* 6: 9–13.

Stone Sweet, A. (1999) 'Judicialization and the Construction of Governance', *Comparative Political Studies* 31: 147–184.

Stone Sweet, A., Grisel, F. (2017) *The Evolution of International Arbitration: Judicialization, Governance, Legitimacy*, Oxford: Oxford University Press.

Strathern, M. (1992a) *Reproducing the Future. Anthropology, Kinship, and the New Reproductive Technologies*, New York: Routledge.

Strathern, M. (1992b) *After Nature: English Kinship in the Late Twentieth Century*, Cambridge: Cambridge University Press.

Strathern, M. (2005) *Kinship, Law and the Unexpected: Relatives are Always a Surprise*, Cambridge: Cambridge University Press.

Stryker, S. (2008) *Transgender History*, Berkeley, CA: Seal Press.

Stychin, C.F. (2009) 'Faith in the Future: Sexuality, Religion and the Public Sphere', *Oxford Journal of Legal Studies* 29: 729–755.

Swennen, F. (ed.) (2015a) *Contractualisation of Family Law – Global Perspectives*, Dordrecht: Springer.

Swennen, F. (2015b) 'Private Ordering in Family Law: A Global Perspective', in Swennen, F. (ed.) *Contractualisation of Family Law – Global Perspectives*, Dordrecht: Springer, pp. 1–59.

Swennen, F., Croce, M. (2016) 'The Symbolic Power of Legal Kinship Terminology: An Analysis of "Co-motherhood" and "Duo-motherhood" in Belgium and the Netherlands', *Social & Legal Studies* 25(2): 181–203.

Swennen, F., Croce, M. (2017) 'Family (Law) Assemblages: New Modes of Being (Legal)', *Journal of Law and Society* 44(4), 532–558.

Tamanaha, B.Z. (2008) 'Understanding Legal Pluralism: Past to Present, Local to Global', *Sydney Law Review* 30: 375–411.

Tate, C.N., Vallinder, T. (eds) (1995) *The Global Expansion of Judicial Power*, New York: New York University Press.

Taylor, C. (2007) *A Secular Age*, Cambridge, MA: Harvard University Press.

Taylor, C. (2009) 'The Polysemy of the Secular', *Social Research* 76: 1143–1166.

Taylor, C. (2010) 'Afterword: Apologia pro Libro suo', in Warner, M., VanAntwerpen, J., Calhoun C.J. (eds), *Varieties of Secularism in a Secular Age*, Cambridge, MA: Harvard University Press, pp. 300–321.

Teubner, G. (ed.) (1987) *Juridification of Social Spheres: A Comparative Analysis in the Areas of Labor, Corporate, Anti-Trust and Social Welfare*, Berlin: Walter de Gruyter.

Théry, I. (1993) *Le Démariage*, Paris: Odile Jacob.

Thomas, Y. (1995) 'Fictio legis. L'empire de la fiction romaine et ses limites médiévales', *Droits, revue française de théorie juridique* 21: 17–63.

Thomas, Y. (2004) '*Res Religiosae*: On the Categories of Religion and Commerce in Roman Law', in Pottage, A., Mundy, M., *Law, Anthropology, and the Constitution of the Social. Making Persons and Things*, Cambridge: Cambridge University Press, pp. 40–72.

Thompson, C. (2001) 'Strategic Naturalizing: Kinship in an Infertility Clinic', in Franklin, S., McKinnon, S. (eds), *Relative Values: Reconfiguring Kinship Studies*, Durham, NC: Duke University Press, pp. 175–202.

Tilly, C. (1989) 'Cities and States in Europe, 1000–1800', *Theory and Society* 5: 563–584.

Turner, B.S., Arslan B.Z. (2011) 'Shari'a and Legal Pluralism in the West', *European Journal of Social Theory* 14(2): 139–159.

Turner, G., Mills, S., van der Bom, I., Coffey-Glover, L., Paterson, L.L., Jones, L. (2017) 'Opposition as Victimhood in Newspaper Debates about Same-sex Marriage', *Discourse & Society*, forthcoming.

Valverde, M. (2006) 'A New Entity in the History of Sexuality. The Respectable Same-Sex Couple', *Feminist Studies* 32(1): 155–162.

van der Veer, P. (2009) 'Spirituality in Modern Society', *Social Research* 76(4): 1097–1120.

van Waarden, F., Hildebrand, Y. (2009) 'From Corporatism to Lawyocracy? On Liberalization and Juridification', *Regulation & Governance* 3: 259–286.

Vatuk, S. (2001) '"Where Will She Go? What Will She Do?": Paternalism Towards Women in the Administration of Muslim Personal Law in Contemporary India', in Larson, G.J. (ed.), *Religion and Personal Law in India*, Bloomington, IN: Indiana University Press, pp. 226–248.

Venditti, V. (2016) 'Millennials Rights: Politics on the Lam', *Politica & Società* 2: 169–188.

Viveiros de Castro, E. (2014) *Cannibal Metaphysics: For a Post-structural Anthropology*, Minneapolis, MN: Univocal.

Warner, M. (1999) *The Trouble with Normal. Sex, Politics, and the Ethics of Queer Life*, Cambridge, MA: Harvard University Press.

Weeks, J. (1990) *Coming Out. Homosexual Politics in Britain from the Nineteenth Century to the Present*, London: Quartet Books.

Weston, K. (1991) *Families We Choose: Lesbians, Gays, Kinship*, New York: Columbia University Press.

Wilkinson, E. (2010) 'What's Queer about Non-monogamy Now?', in Barker, M., Langdridge, D. (eds), *Understanding Non-monogamies*, New York: Routledge, pp. 243–254.

Winch, P. (1964) 'Understanding a Primitive Society', *American Philosophical Quarterly* 1(4): 307–324.

Wittig, M. (1992) *The Straight Mind and Other Essays*, Boston, MA: Beacon Press.

Woltersdorff, V. (2011) 'Paradoxes of Precarious Sexualities. Sexual Sub-cultures under Neo-liberalism', *Cultural Studies* 25(2): 164–182.

Woodman, G.R. (2006) 'The Involvement of English Common Law with Other Laws', in Eberhard, C., Vernicos, G. (eds), *La quête anthropologique du droit: Autour de la démarche d'Étienne Le Roy*, Paris: Éditions Karthala, pp. 477–500.

Woodman, G.R. (2008) 'The Possibilities of Co-existence of Religious Laws with Other Laws', in Mehdi, R., Petersen, H., Reenberg Sand, E., Woodman, G.R. (eds), *Law and Religion in Multicultural Societies*, Copenhagen: DJØF Publishing.

Zion-Waldoks, T. (2015) 'Politics of Devoted Resistance: Agency, Feminism, and Religion among Orthodox Agunah Activists in Israel', *Gender & Society* 29(1): 73–97.

Index

www.ingramcontent.com/pod-product-compliance
Ingram Content Group UK Ltd.
Pitfield, Milton Keynes, MK11 3LW, UK
UKHW020426010325
455677UK00029B/1014